MALAY *in* 3 WEEKS

John Parry
Sahari bin Sulaiman

Times Editions
Marshall Cavendish

New Edition 1985
Reprinted 1986, 1988, 1989, 1990, 1992,
1993, 1995, 1996, 2001, 2005
This edition with new cover 2003

Published by Times Editions – Marshall Cavendish
An imprint of Marshall Cavendish International (Asia) Private Limited
A member of Times Publishing Limited

Times Centre, 1 New Industrial Road, Singapore 536196
Tel: (65) 6213 9288 Fax: (65) 6285 4871
E-mail: te@sg.marshallcavendish.com
Online Book Store: www.marshallcavendish.com/genref

Malaysian Office:
Marshall Cavendish (Malaysia) Sdn Bhd (3024-D)
(Formerly known as Federal Publications Sdn Bhd)
Times Subang, Lot 46, Subang Hi-Tech Industrial Park
Batu Tiga, 40000 Shah Alam, Selangor Darul Ehsan, Malaysia
Tel: (603) 5635 2191, 5628 6888 Fax: (603) 5635 2706
E-mail: cchong@my.marshallcavendish.com

National Library Board (Singapore) Cataloguing in Publication Data

Parry, John, 1927-
Malay in 3 weeks / John Parry, Sahari bin Sulaiman.
– Singapore : Times Editions–Marshall Cavendish, 2005.
p. cm. – (Times learn Malay)
ISBN : 981-232-645-6

1. Malay language – Spoken Malay. 2. Malay language – Conversation and phrase books – English. 3. Malay language – Study and teaching – Foreign speakers. I. Sahari bin Sulaiman. II. Title. III. Series: Times learn Malay
PL5105

499.2882421 — dc21 SLS2005006648

Printed in Singapore by CMO Image Printing Enterprise

CONTENTS

INTRODUCTION

This book is divided into three parts:

a series of ten lessons, the content of which should be easily mastered in three weeks,

a series of ten conversations, each of which deals with a different everyday situation, and which are intended to be used as a phrase book,

a miniature 'dictionary' or vocabulary list.

The language taught in this book is not pure Malay. It is a colloquial development of Malay and is essentially the language which the various communities in Malaysia use when communicating with each other. An example of pure Malay is given in Conversation Ten. In the other Conversations, you will find the kind of Malay which you are most likely to hear and to use.

When you have mastered the contents of this book, you should find no difficulty in making yourself understood, nor in understanding what people say to you.

How to use this book

Part One

There is a short reading passage at the beginning of each lesson (except Lessons 5 and 10). First check the pronunciation, making use of the rules given on page 9. Then, take each sentence in turn and, with the aid of the vocabulary list given in the lesson, translate each sentence 'word-for-word'.

e.g. *Itu meja besar.*
That is a big table.

'Word-for-word' : That table big.

Compare your 'word-for-word' version with the English as given, and you will see how each sentence is constructed. Then check your findings with the notes given with each lesson.

This may seem rather complicated at first, but it will soon prove to be much easier than it appears, as well as being a very interesting way of studying.

Contained in each lesson is an untranslated passage for reading. This is intended to give practice in the language. 'Thinking' in a new language always proves difficult at the start, but it is a habit and, like all habits, it grows with time.

Part Two

This part may either be used as a continuation of Part One, or it may be used as a phrase book. No new grammar is introduced in this part, although some of the sentences are longer. It will easily be seen how they are put together.

After completing Part Two of this book, the learner's next step is to enlarge his vocabulary. The easiest way to learn a large number of words in a short time is the oldest: deliberately learning by heart.

Pronunciation

As with English, the pronunciation of Malay varies according to the part of the country from which the speaker comes. The best way in which to learn how to pronounce a language properly is to listen to a native of the country concerned. Rules of pronunciation are given below, but if you can ask a Malay to read the lessons aloud to you, so much the better.

The form of romanized spelling used in this book is mainly phonetic.

There are none of the variations of 'bough', 'enough' and 'cough' which make English spelling such a nuisance even to natives of England.

Vowels:
a, e, as in *cafe,* with the following exceptions:

a when the final syllable, as in *mana,* is pronounced as the 'er' in the English 'river'.

e is similar to the last 'e' in the English 'beaten'.

i as in the English 'machine'.

o as in English 'joke' — but with the purity of a French 'eau'.

u as the 'oo' in 'fool'.

Diphthongs:

ai as the 'i' in 'mine'; except where there is a slight break in the sound: *la/in:* as in a closed syllable.

au as the 'ow' in 'brown'.

Consonants:

g is always hard, as in 'go'. In the middle of a word, a single 'g' belongs to the preceding syllable: *tang/an.*

gg is harder: *ping/gan.*

k as in English but when it comes at the end of a word it is not pronounced. Its presence there has the effect of indicating a purer preceding vowel sound, and there is usually a break in the voice, as though the word were not complete (a glottal stop): *rokok* = roko'.

ny is a nasal sound as in 'new'.

r is usually sounded, whatever its position in the word: *besar.*

s as in 'silly' and NOT as in 'his'.

The other consonants are pronounced in much the same way as in English.

Warning: The above instructions for pronunciation are considerably simplified, and even in places technically incorrect. They should however be sufficient to guide the reader through the first couple of weeks. A detailed description of pronunciation would be too long for this book —

even if the reader had the patience to wade through it! Remember: to achieve a good accent in Malay, you must *listen to a Malay speaking* and *imitate him.*

Part One

LESSON ONE
The Simple Statement

First read the Malay text aloud in accordance with the pronunciation principles given on the previous pages. When you feel fairly sure that you know how to pronounce the text correctly, you can begin to examine the meaning and the way in which the words are put together. Notice that there are some words used in English which are NOT used in Malay.

Ini meja.
This is a table.
Ini pinggan.
This is a plate.
Ini sekolah.
This is a school.
Ini sekolah kecil.
This is a small school.
Itu pinggan putih.
That is a white plate.
Ini rumah kecil.
This is a small house.
Ini pinggan putih.
This is a white plate.
Ini meja besar.
This is a big table.
Meja itu besar.
That table is big.
Ini cawan biru.
This is a blue cup.
Cawan saya biru.
My cup is blue.

Itu kerusi.
That is a chair.
Itu cawan.
That is a cup.
Itu rumah.
That is a house.
Itu rumah besar.
That is a big house.
Ini cawan biru.
This is a blue cup.
Rumah ini kecil.
This house is small.
Pinggan ini putih.
This plate is white.
Meja ini besar.
This table is big.
Meja besar.
The big table.
Ini cawan saya.
This is my cup.

Vocabulary:

ini	this, these	*cawan*	cup
itu	that, those	*sekolah*	school
saya	I, my, me	*rumah*	house
meja	table	*kecil*	small
kerusi	chair	*besar*	big
pinggan	plate	*putih*	white
biru	blue		

Notes

Compare these notes with the text above:

1. In Malay, there is NO verb 'to be'.
2. The articles *a* and *the* are not used. The word *itu* can be used to point out a particular object or to give a better balance to the sentence.
3. In Malay, the adjective generally follows the noun: the white plate = *pinggan putih*

NO ENGLISH is given for the following passage, but you should be able to understand it with the aid of the additional vocabulary. Check the pronunciation first. Try to understand the meaning of the passage without translating it.

Ini rumah besar. Ini rumah saya. Rumah saya bersih. Lantai itu bersih. Bilik itu bersih. Bilik itu tak kotor. Cawan itu kotor. Piring itu bersih. Cawan putih itu kotor. Cawan biru itu bersih. Piring merah itu bersih. Piring putih itu kotor. Rumah saya bersih. Cawan saya kotor. Pinggan saya bersih.

Additional vocabulary:

merah	red	*lantai*	floor
bersih	clean	*piring*	saucer, small plate
kotor	dirty		
bilik	room	*tak* or *tidak*	no, not

LESSON TWO
Asking a Question

First check the pronunciation carefully, reading the passage aloud. Then examine the meaning and the structure of the sentences.

Apa itu?
What is that?
Itu kerusi.
That is a chair.
Apa ini?
What is this?
Ini meja.
This is a table.
Adakah meja itu besar?
Is it a big table?
Itu meja besar.
It is a big table.
Tidak, itu meja kecil.
No, it is a small table.
Ada berapa buah kerusi?
How many chairs are there?
Ada dua buah kerusi.
There are two chairs.
Mem ada berapa banyak rumah?
How many houses have you, madam/ma'am?
Saya ada sebuah rumah.
I have one house.
Ada berapa biji cawan dan piring?
How many cups and saucers are there?

Ada lima biji cawan dan empat biji piring.
There are five cups and four saucers.
Berapa harga sebuah pinggan?
How much does a plate cost?
Satu ringgit sebuah.
One dollar each.
Kasi saya empat.
Give me four.
Berapa harga sekilogram daging ini?
How much a kilogramme is this meat?
Dua ringgit sekilogram.
Two dollars a kilogramme.

Vocabulary:

se, satu	one	*adakah*	is it that? cf. *est-ce que,* in French
dua	two	*dan*	and
tiga	three	*ringgit*	dollar
empat	four	*kilogram*	kilogramme
lima	five	*buah*	fruit (see note 3)
apa?	what?	*biji*	seed (see note 3)
berapa?	how much? how many?	*daging*	meat
banyak	much, many	*kasi*	give
berapa banyak	how many?	*mem*	Usual form of address for non-Malay women (see Lesson Five)
harga	price	*ada*	have; there is; there are; (as a question), are there? etc.
berapa harga?	how much? what price?		

Notes:

1. *Adakah:* this question form is both common and useful. Generally, *adakah* will indicate some form of possession: *Adakah meja itu besar?* Is it that this table is big? or Does this table possess bigness? Hence, is it a big table?
2. It: notice how the word 'it' is avoided in the above

sentences, the subject being directly approached.

3. In Malay, one does not speak of 'one chair' but of 'one piece of chair'. There must always be a classifying word. *Buah* is used for most larger objects: *dua buah kerusi* = two (pieces of) chair(s). *Biji* is for all smaller objects. This may appear difficult, but in fact it is extremely easy if the classifier is learnt with the noun. See Lesson Five.

As you will notice with the cups and saucers of this lesson, *buah* and *biji* are sometimes interchangeable with doubtful objects.

Read the following passage aloud. TRY TO UNDERSTAND IT WITHOUT TRANSLATION. Only translate as a last resort.

Ini rumah saya. Itu rumah elok. Saya ada sebuah rumah. Saya ada tiga buah meja. Meja-meja[1] *itu besar. Kasi saya dua buah kerusi. Adakah cawan itu hitam? Tidak, cawan itu biru. Adakah cawan itu cantik? Ia, cawan biru itu cantik. Ada berapa buah cawan biru? Ada lima buah cawan biru dan lima buah piring biru. Ada berapa buah pinggan? Ada tiga buah pinggan. Ada tiga biji buah nenas.*

Additional Vocabulary:

hitam	black	*elok*	fine
buah nenas	pineapple	*cantik*	pretty
ia	yes		

[1]Meja-meja: table: a repetition of nouns sometimes, but not always, indicates a plural. Be careful with this: sometimes the meaning changes, cf. *mata* = eye; *mata-mata* = policeman.

LESSON THREE
Numbers to One Hundred

Examine the following passage as in the previous lessons:—

Ahmad ada lima puluh ringgit lima puluh sen.
Ahmad has fifty dollars fifty cents.
Husain ada lima ringgit dua puluh sen.
Husain has five dollars twenty cents.
Saya ada enam ringgit tujuh puluh sen.
I have six dollars seventy cents.
Dia ada empat ringgit empat belas sen.
He has four dollars fourteen cents.
Ada lapan orang laki-laki.
There are eight men.
Ada lapan belas orang.
There are eighteen people.
Ada lapan puluh orang laki-laki dan lapan puluh orang perempuan.
There are eighty men and eighty women.
Dua orang laki-laki itu makan buah.
Those two men are eating fruit.
Apa tiga orang perempuan itu makan?
What are those three women eating?
Dia orang makan telur.
They are eating eggs.
Ada berapa orang kanak-kanak?
How many children are there?
Ada satu ratus orang kanak-kanak.
There are one hundred children.
Ada berapa kereta?
How many cars are there?

Ada sepuluh kereta.
There are ten cars.

Vocabulary:

enam	six	*lima belas*	15
tujuh	seven	*ratus*	hundred
lapan	eight	*sen*	cent
sembilan	nine	*dia*	he, she
puluh	(a multiple ten)	*dia orang*	they (of persons)
sepuluh	10	*laki-laki*	male (of persons)
dua puluh	20		
tujuh puluh dua	72	*perempuan*	female (-do-)
belas	-teen (in numbers)	*kanak-kanak*	child
		kereta	motor car
sebelas	11	*makan*	eat
dua belas	12	*telur*	egg
orang	people		

Notes:

1. The note at the end of Lesson Two mentions the possibility of doubling a noun to indicate a plural: e.g. *meja-meja* = tables. Normally, however, the noun need not change when there is some other word, such as a number, which will serve the same purpose. Cf. the sentences above.
2. The formation of numbers up to 100 follows the lines indicated in the text and vocabulary of this lesson.
3. Many words are used with great flexibility. e.g. *makan* may be 'to eat' or 'a meal'. In good Malay *makan* would be subject to prefixes, such as *memakan* = to eat, or suffixes, such as *makanan* = a meal; but the rules governing the use of these are too complicated to be within the scope of this course.
4. *Orang* is used for 'people'. *Orang laki-laki* = men. *Orang perempuan* = women. *Dua orang budak* = two children.

Read the following passage aloud. Try to understand it without translation.

Saya ada tiga orang anak: dua orang laki-laki dan satu orang perempuan. Hari-hari dia orang suka main bola. Dia orang makan apa? Dia orang makan buah nenas. Awak ada berapa orang anak? Saya ada tiga orang anak, sembilan buah kerusi, empat buah meja, sebiji buah nenas dan seorang suami.

Additional Vocabulary:

anak	child, offspring	*awak*	you (see Lesson Five)
suka	like	*bola*	ball
main	play	*hari*	day
suami	husband	*hari-hari*	every day
nenas	pineapple		

LESSON FOUR
Some Verbs

Examine the following passage as in the previous lessons:—

Mrs. Smith:	*John, mari sini! Engkau main apa?*
	John, come here! What are you playing?
John:	*Saya main bola.*
	I'm playing ball.
Mrs. Smith:	*Engkau mahu makan buah betik?*
	Would you like to eat some papaya?
	Nanti. Cuci tangan engkau dahulu.
	Wait. You must first wash your hands.
Mrs. Smith:	*Engkau suka tak buah betik itu?*
	Do you like the papaya?
	Sedap tak?
	Is it good?
John:	*Ia, sedap.*
	Yes, it's fine.
Mrs. Smith:	*Pinggan itu kotor. Pergi cucikan.*
	That plate is dirty. Go and wash it.
John:	*Baiklah!*
	O.K.

Vocabulary:

mari	come here!	*cucikan*	wash (see note 3)
mahu	want, like, wish	*pergi*	go
		nanti	wait
buah betik	papaya	*tangan*	hand
sedap	tasty, good (food)	*dahulu*	first, before
		baik	good, all right
sini	here	*engkau*	you (when an older

lah	(a suffix used to emphasise the word to which it is attached)	person speaks to a younger one) see Lesson Five

Notes:

1. *Mari* is used in the sense of 'come here' or 'coming towards'. Note also the use 'let us . . .' e.g. *mari, pergi:* come, let's go.
2. 'Like' in the sense of want is *mahu;* in the sense of 'enjoy' it is *suka.*
3. *kan:* this suffix has various uses. It is not intended to teach these uses in this course. You will often hear it used as above, where it implies an order.
4. *Tidak:* is often used with the sense 'don't you?' Cf. above *Engkau suka tak betik itu?* Literally, 'You like, don't you, that papaya?'

Read the following passage aloud. Try to understand it without translation.

Saya ada sebuah rumah elok. Ada kebun dan lima buah bilik. Saya tak suka cuci pinggan, tapi saya suka cuci kain. Mula-mula saya mahu sabun. Air panas baik. Air sejuk tak baik. Anak-anak[1] *saya minum air susu, tapi saya minum teh dan kopi.*

Additional Vocabulary:

air	water	*kebun*	garden
air susu	milk	*cuci pinggan*	to wash dishes
(air) teh	tea	*cuci kain*	to wash clothes
(air) kopi	coffee	*sabun*	soap
minum	drink	*panas*	hot
tapi	but	*sejuk*	cold
mula-mula	firstly		

[1]The plural again

LESSON FIVE
Revision, Pronouns, Classifiers, Titles

Revision:
In the preceding four lessons you have learned how to make a simple statement and how to ask a simple question. Go over again the reading passages in each of the four lessons.

Pronouns:
'I': The usual pronoun for 'I' is *saya.* Note that Malays will sometimes use their own names in place of the pronoun.
'you': There is a large number of words meaning 'you'. When speaking to a servant, it is usual to use the person's proper name in place of the pronoun. The servant will normally address you as *mem* or *tuan.* To a Malay stranger, use *encik.* To a Malay of high social class, *tuan* is usual. *Engkau* is a familiar term (cf. French 'tu'), used by a superior to an inferior, as in Lesson Four when a mother is speaking to her son. *Awak* is generally used when speaking to equals.
'he', 'she': *Dia,* sometimes used in the form *ia.*
'we': Again, there is a certain amount of variety. Generally, *kita.*
'you' (plural): As in singular.
'they': *Dia orang* is most common in conversation.
Note: The rules governing the use of various personal pronouns, and even the pronouns themselves, vary from one district to another. Study the practice of your own area.

Classifiers (or Numeral Co-efficients):
Many Europeans try to avoid the use of these. You will, however, hear them constantly used, and they are not difficult to learn. Here are six common classifiers:

buah:	larger objects (when not covered by another classifier)
biji:	smaller objects
orang:	human beings
ekor:	living creatures other than humans
batang:	rod-like things, such as walking sticks, pencils, trees
bilah:	knives and other objects with blades: e.g. spears

Titles:
Tuan and *mem* are used for Mr. and Mrs. (non-Malays). For Malays *Encik* is used for men and *Cik* for women, *Tuan* for men and *Puan* for married women.

Vocabulary:

ekor	tail	*tuan*	master, Mr.
batang	rod, shaft, handle, tree-trunk	*encik*	Mr.
		cik	Miss
bilah	bar (of a cage)	*puan*	Mrs. (married woman)

Exercises:
1. Translate into Malay:

Have you any money? How much money have you? Do you smoke cigarettes, Ahmad? Are there many pineapples? Are there many bananas? How much are potatoes a kilogramme? I have twenty-nine potatoes. There are knives, forks and spoons. I want to buy three knives. I don't like washing clothes.
(There is a suggested translation on page 99.)

Additional Vocabulary (1):

duit/wang	money	*ubi kentang*	potato
rokok	cigarette	*pisau*	knife
hisap rokok	to smoke	*garpu*	fork
pisang	banana	*sudu*	spoon
beli	buy		

2. Read the following passage for practice:

Saya suka makan buah. Saya mahu beli buah betik, buah nenas, buah pisang dan buah kelapa. Anak-anak saya tak mahu tidur. Dia orang mahu main bola. Suami saya suka hisap rokok. Awak ada jual rokok? Awak ada jual roti? Saya mahu gula. Saya tak mahu garam. Cawan ini retak, yang itu pecah. Saya suka bunga kuning.

Additional Vocabulary (2):

kelapa	coconut	*gula*	sugar
tidur	sleep	*garam*	salt
jual	sell	*retak*	cracked
roti	bread	*pecah*	broken (smashed)
yang itu	that one, those	*bunga*	flower
yang ini	this one, these	*kuning*	yellow

LESSON SIX
In, On, Where is?

Examine the following passage as in the previous lessons:—

Ada lima orang di dalam kebun.
There are five people in the garden.
Ada dua orang budak-budak di dalam rumah.
There are two children in the house.
Ada enam puluh tujuh ekor anjing di dalam Kebun Bunga.
There are sixty-seven dogs in the Botanic Gardens.
Ada satu biji ubi kentang di dalam bakul.
There is one potato in the basket.
Awak ada berapa biji telur?
How many eggs have you?
Saya ada seratus biji telur di dalam bakul saya.
I have one hundred eggs in my basket.
Saya ada tiga biji telur di dalam pinggan.
I have three eggs on the plate.
Saya ada tiga telur goreng di dalam pinggan.
I have three fried eggs on my plate.
Pinggan saya biru.
My plate is blue.
Tiga biji telur saya itu putih dan kuning.
My three eggs are white and yellow.
Saya suka makan telur.
I like eating eggs.
Saya mahu makan tiga biji telur.
I want to eat three eggs.
Berapa biji telur boleh saya makan?
How many eggs can I eat?

Vocabulary:

di dalam	in	*anjing*	dog
di atas	on	*bakul*	basket
budak	young boy or girl	*goreng*	fry
		boleh	to be able

Notes:

1. *Di dalam* (in) and *di atas* (on): The *di* may be used by itself to indicate position: e.g. *di rumah* = in the house. *Di* always indicates place. You will notice that in Lesson 9 *di mana* = what place; and *ke mana* = where to? Both may be translated into English as 'where'.
2. *Tiga biji telur saya itu putih dan kuning.*: the word *itu* in this sentence adds a stress, drawing attention to particular eggs.
3. *Main-main* in the passage below means 'playing' in general. The word *main* is usually used singly in connection with a particular game: e.g. *main bola* to play ball; *main rugbi* to play rugby.

Try to understand the following passage without translating it:

Di mana awak? Saya di dalam kebun. Di mana budak-budak? Budak-budak di dalam bilik tidur. Apa dia orang buat di dalam bilik tidur? Dia orang tidur. Adakah dia orang suka tidur? Tidak, dia orang suka main-main. Adakah dia suka main-main? Kadang-kadang. Awak suka apa? Saya suka tidur. Di mana awak? Saya duduk di atas kerusi. Di mana kerusi itu? Di dalam bilik ini. Di mana bilik itu? Di dalam rumah saya. Di mana rumah awak? Di Singapura.

Additional Vocabulary (1):

di mana	where is?	*kadang-kadang*	sometimes
bilik tidur	bedroom	*duduk*	sit, dwell
buat	do	*Singapura*	Singapore

Additional Vocabulary (2):

Some divisions of time:—

pagi	morning	*hari ini*	today
tengahari	midday, early afternoon	*esok*	tomorrow
		minggu	week
petang	late afternoon, evening	*bulan*	month, moon
		tahun	year
malam	night		
semalam	yesterday		

LESSON SEVEN
Time

Examine the following passage:

Pukul berapa? Pukul lapan.
What time is it? Eight o'clock.
Pukul berapa makan malam? Pukul tujuh setengah.
What time is dinner? (At) half past seven.
Tolong datang pukul enam suku.
Please come at a quarter past six.
Saya datang pukul enam pagi atau petang?
Shall I come at 6 o'clock in the morning or 6 o'clock in the evening?
Pukul berapa? Saya tak tahu. Saya tak ada jam.
What time is it? I don't know. I haven't a watch.
Ada jam gantung di dalam bilik itu.
There's a clock in that room.
Saya mahu jam tangan.
I should like to have a wrist watch.
Malam ini kita makan daging kambing.
Today we're having lamb for dinner.
Semalam kita makan daging lembu.
Yesterday we had beef (for dinner).
Esok kita makan daging babi.
Tomorrow we shall have pork.
Kita makan daging tiap-tiap hari. Saya pergi kerja tiap-tiap pagi.
We eat meat every day. I go to work every morning.
Saya tidur tiap-tiap malam.
I sleep every night.
Saya minum teh tiap-tiap tengahari.
I drink tea every afternoon.

Sudah pukul empat. Saya mesti keluar.
It's already 4 o'clock. I must go out.

Vocabulary:

pukul	strike, o'clock	*gantung*	hanging, suspended
makan malam	dinner	*kambing*	sheep, goat
		lembu	cow, bull, ox
setengah	half	*esok*	tomorrow
tolong	please, help	*babi*	pig
datang	come	*tiap-tiap*	every
suku	quarter	*kerja*	work
kah	(interrogative suffix)	*tengah*	middle (see *setengah,* above)
tahu	know	*sudah*	done, finished
jam	clock; hour	*mesti*	must
keluar	to go out		

Notes:

1. It will be seen from the above that the method of telling the time is simple. Two points should be noticed: when the time is 'past' the hour, then begin with *pukul* (e.g. *pukul enam sepuluh minit* = ten past six); but when the time is 'to' the hour, then begin with *kurang* e.g. *kurang lima minit pukul lapan* = five to eight). Here are some time words which are not in the vocabulary:—

   minit minute *kurang* less, reduction

2. *kah* is a suffix indicating a sense of doubt. It is always used interrogatively.
3. Meat: The word for meat is *daging.* The kind of meat is indicated by adding an extra word: *daging lembu* = beef; *daging kambing* = lamb or mutton.

Translate the following into Malay:

What time is it? I drink tea every day. He is coming at half-past six. Tonight we are having pork for dinner. Please come at ten past six. Please come at five to eight. I do not like working. I like playing. I have two eggs. How many eggs have you? (There is a suggested translation on page 99.)

LESSON EIGHT
ke and nya

Examine the following passage:

Esok pagi saya akan pergi ke sekolah.
Tomorrow morning I shall go to school.
Di sekolah itu ada tiga puluh orang kanak-kanak dan seorang guru.
In that school there are thirty children and one teacher.
Guru itu tua.
The teacher is old.
Sekolah itu sudah lama.
The school is old.
Guru itu enam puluh tahun umurnya.
The teacher is sixty years old.
Sekolah itu sudah seratus tahun umurnya.
The school is one hundred years old.
Umur saya dua belas tahun. Saya tidak tua. Saya muda.
I am twelve years old. I am not old. I am young.
Mari sini. Pergi sana. Bangun. Duduk.
Come here. Go there. Stand up. Sit down.
Ini gayanya guru itu cakap.
This is the way the teacher speaks.

Vocabulary:

akan	shall (indicates intention)	*nya*	suffix indicating possession
guru	teacher	*muda*	young
tua	old,	*sana*	there
lama	old, ancient, long (of time)	*bangun*	stand up
		gaya	manner, tone

umur	age	*cakap*	speak

Notes:

1. *ke* is a prefix used to mean 'towards', as in the first sentence above.
2. *nya:* indicates possession: e.g. *orang itu dan keretanya* = the man and his car. Note the use of this suffix in various contexts throughout this book. It will be seen that it is more frequent than similar possessive words in English: e.g. note in Conversation Six (page 56) Mrs. Smith's second speech.
3. In sentence six on page 31, *sudah* gives the idea of 'already'.

Try to understand the following passage without translating it:

Bawakan saya cawan lain. Ambil piring ini. Suruh drebar belok kanan. Suruh drebar belok kiri. Tolong belok kanan. Tolong belok kiri. Tolong berhenti di sini. Sila masuk. Saya suka baca. Saya tak suka tulis. Ada lima buah buku di dalam almari.

Additional Vocabulary:

bawa	bring	*sila*	please (indicating welcome)
lain	other, another	*berhenti*	stop
ambil	take away	*masuk*	come in
suruh	tell, give an order	*baca*	read
belok	turn	*tulis*	write
kanan	right	*buku*	book
kiri	left	*almari*	cupboard
tolong	please (when giving an instruction)	*drebar*	driver

(NB. With *ambilkan* the suffix *kan* does not indicate a command. Instead, it changes the meaning to 'bring'.)

LESSON NINE
Where to?

Examine the following passage:

Di mana beg tangan awak?
Where is your handbag?
Pagi tadi ada di atas meja.
This morning it was on the table.
Tolong carikan.
Please look for it.
Saya tak nampak beg itu tengahari ini.
I did not see it this afternoon.
Apa ada dalam beg itu?
What was in the bag?
Saya punya saputangan, gincu, kotak bedak, sedikit duit, cermin muka, kotak rokok, dan pemetikapi.
My handkerchief, lipstick, powder compact, some money, a mirror, cigarette case, and cigarette lighter.
Ini dia beg tangan awak.
Here is your handbag.
Di bawah kerusi ini.
It was under this chair.
Saya mesti keluar pada pukul empat.
I must go out at four o'clock.
Awak mahu pergi ke mana.
Where are you going.
Saya mahu pergi tengok wayang gambar.
I'm going to the cinema.
Jangan lupa bawa cerminmata.
(Then) don't forget to take your glasses (spectacles).

Apa nama filem itu?
What's the name of the film?
"Seribu Satu Malam."
"A Thousand and One Nights."
Adakah awak mahu bawa kereta?
Are you going to take the car?
Ia, tapi saya tak pakai drebar.
Yes, but I shan't need the driver.
Tidak, saya pergi naik bus.
No, I shall go by bus.
Saya akan balik naik teksi.
I shall return by taxi.

Vocabulary:

di mana	where is	*bawah*	under(neath)
ke mana	where to	*pada*	by, at, near, in
tadi	recently (indicates immediate past)	*tengok*	look at, see
cari	look for	*wayang*	a theatrical performance
nampak	see, be visible	*gambar*	picture
punya	own (indicating possession)	*wayang gambar*	pictures/cinema
saputangan	handkerchief	*jangan*	don't (forbidding)
kotak	chest, locker, packet, container	*lupa*	forget
bedak	cosmetic powder	*mata*	eye
sedikit	small, little	*cerminmata*	glasses
cermin	mirror	*mata-mata*	policeman
muka	face	*nama*	name
gincu	lipstick	*ribu*	thousand
pemetikapi	lighter	*pakai*	make use of
		naik	to mount, go up, get up into
		balik	return

Notes:

1. The Malay language is rapidly absorbing a large number of English words, mainly in connection with modern inventions or European habits and customs. These words are not included in the vocabulary lists, nor in the index at the end of this book unless the spelling has been changed: e.g. *stoking.*

2. The word *sapu* really gives the idea of wiping. Note here *saputangan* = handkerchief.

3. The word *bawa* can also be used for the English to 'drive' a car.

4. *Naik* is used when motion upwards is indicated. Notice the following.

naik basikal:	to go on a bicycle
naik tangga:	to go upstairs
naik pangkat:	to be promoted

Translate the following into Malay:

Where is your handkerchief? Where are you going? Are you going to the Botanic Gardens today? No, I am going to the pictures. Please bring a cup of milk. Please take this cup of water away. This morning there were two people in this room. Please look for my handbag. Please come in. Tell him to turn left.

(There is a suggested translation on page 99.)

LESSON TEN
Days of the Week; Tense

Revision:
Note the three prepositions *ke* (to, towards), *di* (at, on, in), and *dari* (from). The first two are always combined with other words indicating place or position, as shown in the text of the preceding lessons and the following ten 'Conversations'. The third, *dari*, may be used as an individual word. Note also the possible combinations with such nouns of position as *atas* (top), *bawah* (under) and *balik* (reverse). NOTE THE WAY THEY ARE USED IN THE TEXT.

Days of the Week:

Monday	*hari satu*	*hari Isnin*
Tuesday	*hari dua*	*hari Selasa*
Wednesday	*hari tiga*	*hari Rabu*
Thursday	*hari empat*	*hari Khamis*
Friday	*hari lima*	*hari Jumaat*
Saturday	*hari enam*	*hari Sabtu*
Sunday	*hari minggu*	*hari Ahad*

Note: The names given in the third column are seldom used or understood by non-Malays.

Tense:
There is no tense in Malay as one knows it in European languages. The subtleties of the Malay verb are difficult to summarise under easy headings, and in any case they would be far beyond the scope of this course. Briefly, when time past or future is to be expressed, it is usually indicated by means of an extra word. A word frequently used to indicate

past tense is *sudah,* giving the idea that the action is complete. For the future, *akan* is common for showing intention. Frequently, however, a mention of the time (such as *semalam* or *esok)* is sufficient to show whether the action is in the future or the past.

Exercise:

Try to understand the following passage without translating it:—

Awak mahu pergi ke mana, Ahmad? Saya tak pergi ke mana-mana. Tolong carikan cerminmata hitam saya. Awak letak di mana? Saya sudah lupa di mana saya letak. Pukul berapa awak balik semalam? Lebih kurang pukul tiga dua puluh minit. Awak pakai cerminmata hitam itu tak? Ia, saya pakai. Saya nampak awak di Sekolah Gambar semalam, tapi saya tak nampak awak pakai cerminmata itu.

Vocabulary:

dari	from	*letak*	put, keep
balik	return	*lebih*	more, greater
mana-mana	anywhere	*lebih kurang*	more or less
cerminmata hitam	sun-glasses	*Sekolah Gambar*	Museum

Translate into Malay:

Where are you going to John? I have forgotten my sun-glasses. Please look for my cigarette case. Do you like playing? Sometimes. How many cups and saucers are there? How much does a plate cost? I have nine children, one chair, two tables, twenty pineapples and two bicycles. Do you like these bananas? Are they good? Please bring me some hot water.
(There is a suggested translation on page 99.)

Part Two

CONVERSATION ONE
Chocolates and Cigarettes

Mrs. Smith: *Selamat pagi, Aminah.*
Good morning, Aminah.

Aminah: *Selamat pagi, mem.*
Good morning, ma'am.
Orang itu sudah lupa lagi bawa suratkhabar.
The man has forgotten to bring the newspaper again.

Mrs. Smith: *Nanti saya cakap.*
I shall speak to him.
Saya mahu keluar sekarang.
I am going out now.
Saya mahu pergi kedai.
I want to go shopping.
Kalau siapa-siapa datang, katakan saya akan balik pukul sebelas.
If anyone comes say that I shall be back at eleven.

Aminah: *Baiklah!*
All right!

(At the shop)

Mrs. Smith: *Selamat pagi.*
Good morning.
Saya mahu beli rokok.
I want to buy cigarettes.
Kasi saya dua karton.
Give me two cartons.

	Bukan, bukan cap ini, cap itu.
	No, not this brand, that one.
Shopkeeper:	*Ada lain-lain apa lagi mem mahu?*
	Is there anything else you want?
Mrs. Smith:	*Saya mahu kertas tulis.*
	I want some writing paper.
	Berapa harga sebuah buku kertas tulis?
	How much is a pad of writing paper?
Shopkeeper:	*Satu ringgit setengah.*
	One dollar fifty.
Mrs. Smith:	*Itu banyak mahal.*
	That is too much.
	Saya kasi lapan puluh sen.
	I'll give you eighty cents.
Shopkeeper:	*Tak boleh, mem. Saya rugi.*
	I can't, ma'am. I would lose (money).
	Apa lagi mem mahu?
	What else do you want?
Mrs. Smith:	*Saya mahu sebotol dakwat.*
	I want one bottle of ink.
	Bukan, dakwat hitam, bukan biru.
	No, black ink, not blue.
	Baiklah, dakwat biru tua.
	All right, blue-black ink.
	Saya mahu buku kecil.
	(And) I want a small note-book.
	Ada buku peringatan untuk lain tahun?
	Have you any diaries for next year?
Shopkeeper:	*Esok baharu ada.*
	Tomorrow I shall have some.
	Ada lain-lain apa lagi mem mahu?
	Anything else you want?
Mrs. Smith:	*Itu sahaja. Terimakasih. Berapa itu?*
	That's all. Thank you. How much is that?
Shopkeeper:	*Mem mahu kertas tulis juga?*
	Do you want the writing paper as well?

Mrs. Smith:	*Tidak. Awak jual banyak mahal.* No. You charge too much.
Shopkeeper:	*Saya kasi mem satu ringgit dua puluh sen.* I'll give it to you for one dollar twenty cents.
Mrs. Smith:	*Baiklah! Berapa semua sekali?* All right! How much is that altogether?
Shopkeeper:	*Empat ringgit sembilan puluh sen.* Four dollars ninety cents.

Vocabulary:

selamat pagi	good morning	*suratkhabar*	newspaper
		sekarang	now
kedai	shop	*pergi kedai*	to go shopping
siapa	who	*siapa-siapa*	anybody
kalau	if	*bukan*	no (contradicting)
cap	brand, make		
lain-lain	anything	*lagi*	more
kertas	paper	*mahal*	costly, dear
rugi	lose	*botol*	bottle
dakwat	ink	*tua*	deep (of colour)
biru tua	blue-black	*untuk*	for
buku peringatan	diary	*terima*	receive, obtain
		terimakasih	thank you
sahaja (NB *itu sahaja* =	only that's all)	*juga*	all the same, and yet, still, to some extent
semua	all, the whole of	*sekali*	once, all at once
		kali	time, occasion
jual	sell	*kasi*	give

Additional Vocabulary:

The following words are not used in the above text, but they may prove useful:—

mata pen	nib	*kayu*	wood
satar	a stroke, a line	*getah*	rubber
		kayu satar	ruler

getah padam	india rubber	*kertas tekap*	blotting paper
padam	extinguish, put out	*tekap*	to rest the flat of the hand over anything, as over a child's mouth to prevent him from speaking; to blot with a pad.
coklat	chocolate		
gula-gula	a sweet		
manis	sweet (of taste)		
pahit	bitter		

CONVERSATION TWO
Buying Vegetables

Seller 1:	*Selamat pagi, mem.*
	Good morning, ma'am.
	Eh, mem! Mahu beli ubi kentang?
	Eh, ma'am! You want to buy potatoes?
Seller 2:	*Eh, mem! Selamat pagi, mem!*
	Eh, ma'am! Good morning, ma'am!
	Ubi kentang, kobis? Saya jual banyak murah!
	Potatoes, cabbages? I sell very cheap!
Mrs. Smith:	*Ubi kentang berapa sekilogram?*
	How much are the potatoes a kilogramme?
Seller 2:	*Tiga puluh sen sekilogram! Banyak murah!*
	Thirty cents a kilogramme! Very cheap!
	Mem mahu satu kilogram! Dua kilogram!
	You want one kilogramme? Two kilogrammes?
	Berapa kilogram mem mahu?
	How much do you want?
Mrs. Smith:	*Itu banyak mahal.*
	That is very dear.
	Ada ubi kentang yang kurang baik.
	Some of these potatoes are not too good.
Seller 2:	*Saya kasi bagus-bagus.*
	I give you good ones.
	Berapa kilogram mem mahu?
	How much ma'am want?
Mrs. Smith:	*Banyak mahal.*
	They're too dear.
Seller 2:	*Baiklah! Saya kasi harga patut, mem.*
	All right! I give you special price.

	Kita kawan-kawan.
	You are my friend.
	Isteri saya tak makan. Saya punya anak . . .
	My wife starves. My little children . . .
Seller 1:	(laughing) *Dia punya anak!*
	His little children!
	Mem, dia tak ada isteri, tak ada anak.
	Ma'am, he has no wife, no children.
Seller 2:	*Harga patut, mem.*
	Special price for you.
	Dua puluh lima sen sekilogram.
	Twenty-five cents a kilogramme.
	Berapa kilogram mahu?
	How many kilogrammes you want?
Mrs. Smith:	*Kasi dua kilogram.*
	Give me two kilogrammes.
Seller 1:	*Eh, mem!*
	Eh, ma'am!
	Mahu, pisang, betik, kelapa, manggis, tomato, epal, limau, durian.
	You like bananas, papayas, coconut, mangosteen, tomatoes, apples, oranges, durian.
Seller 2:	*Mem tak suka durian.*
	Madam does not like durians.
	Orang putih tak makan durian.
	Europeans don't eat durians.
Mrs. Smith:	*Kasi dua kilogram.*
	Give me two kilogrammes.
	Saya suka cuba. Berapa harga?
	I'd like to try. How much is it?
Seller 1:	*Patut, patut, mem.*
	Special price, ma'am.
	Enam puluh sen sekilogram.
	Sixty cents a kilogramme.
Mrs. Smith:	*Baiklah!*
	All right!

Vocabulary:

kobis	cabbage	*manggis*	mangosteen
murah	cheap	*limau*	orange, lemon, lime
kurang baik	not too good		
patut	right, proper	*orang putih*	European
isteri	wife	*bagus*	good
kawan	companion, friend, large group or party.	*pernah*	ever
		tak pernah	never
		rasa	taste, flavour
		cuba	try

Additional Vocabulary:

The following extra words may be useful:

mangga	mango	*lobak merah*	carrot
nangka	jack fruit	*kacang panjang*	long beans
semangka	water melon	*kacang bendi*	ladies finger
ubi kayu	tapioca	*kacang parang*	sword beans
timun	cucumber	*terung*	brinjals
keledek	sweet potato	*kacang boncis*	French beans
keladi	coco-yam		
sengkuang	turnip		
bayam	spinach		
taugih	bean sprouts		
lobak putih	radish		

Rubber		Rice	
kebun getah	rubber estate	*nasi*	cooked rice
bangsal	coolie lines, shed	*sawah*	paddy field
toreh getah	rubber tapping	*padi*	unhusked rice
susu getah	latex	*batas*	bank, ridge around wet paddy field
pokok getah	rubber tree	*sabit*	sickle
		beras	uncooked rice, without the husk

CONVERSATION THREE
Meat and Groceries

Mrs. Smith: *Awak ada jual daging?*
Do you sell meat?

Shopkeeper: *Ia, mem mahu daging apa?*
Yes, what kind do you want?
Daging lembu? Daging kambing?
Beef? Lamb?

Mrs. Smith: *Ada daging babi, tak?*
Have you any pork?

Shopkeeper: *Babi cincang? Ham? Ini bagus.*
Pork chops? Ham? This is a good piece.

Mrs. Smith: *Ini daging Australia?*
Is it Australian meat?

Shopkeeper: *Tidak, ini daging potong di sini.*
No, it was slaughtered locally.
Berapa banyak mem mahu?
How much do you want?

Mrs. Smith: *Kasi saya empat keping daging kambing dan setengah kilogram daging sup lembu.*
Give me four lamb chops and half a kilogramme of stewing beef.

Shopkeeper: *Ada apa lagi mem mahu?*
Anything else you want?
Ada ayam, itik, angsa, ayam belanda, apa-apa mem suka?
We have chicken, duck, goose, turkey, anything you like?

Mrs. Smith: *Awak ada jual bakon?*
Do you sell bacon?

Shopkeeper: *Berapa banyak bakon mem mahu?*
How much bacon do you want?
Nanti saya ambil.
I'll get it for you.
Kedai abang saya di sebelah.
My brother's shop is next door.

Mrs. Smith: *Saya mesti tengok dahulu.*
I must see it first.
Saya akan pergi ke kedai abang awak.
I shall go to your brother's shop.

(In the brother's shop)

Mrs. Smith: *Itu bakon sahaja awak ada?*
Is that the only bacon you've got?

Brother: *Ini bakon baik.*
It is very good bacon.

Mrs. Smith: *Banyak lemak. Saya mahu isi.*
It is too fat. I want lean bacon.

Brother: *Saya ada lagi satu. Boleh tak?*
I have another piece here. Is this all right?
Saya akan potong, tipis atau tebal?
How shall I cut it, thin or thick?

Mrs. Smith: *Tolong potong tipis-tipis. Ada telur tak?*
Please cut it very thin. Have you any eggs?

Brother: *Telur, mentega, marjerin, minyak babi, minyak makan, jem, jem limau, madu. Semua mem mahu ada.*
Eggs, butter, margarine, lard, cooking oil, jam, marmalade, honey. Everything you want.

Mrs. Smith: *Saya mahu enam biji telur.*
I want half a dozen eggs.
Telur-telur ini sangat kecil.
These eggs are very small.

Brother: *Ini telur sangat bagus. Mem mahu dua belas biji?*
These are very good eggs. Will you have twelve?

Mrs. Smith:	*Tidak.* No. *Saya mahu enam biji. Beri saya satu tin mentega setengah kilogram.* I want six. And give me one 500 g tin of butter. *Itu sahaja.* That's all, thank you.

Vocabulary:

cincang	a cut, cutting, slashing	*itik*	duck
potong	to cut off	*angsa*	goose
keping	(classifier for flat objects)	*ayam belanda*	turkey
ayam	chicken, hen, fowl	*abang*	elder brother
isi	content, filling	*sebelah*	side
tipis	thin	*lemak*	fat, grease
tebal	thick	*minyak*	oil, fat
atau	or	*minyak babi*	lard
tipis-tipis	(duplication of an adjective often indicates 'very')	*minyak makan*	cooking oil
mentega	butter	*madu*	honey
apa-apa	whatever	*yang*	(indicates connection between preceding and succeeding words)

Additional Vocabulary:

The following extra words may be useful:

ikan	fish	*penyu*	turtle
ikan yu	dog fish, shark	*kura-kura*	tortoise
ikan sembilang	cat fish	*mutiara*	pearl
ikan pari	sting ray	*ikan tenggiri*	mackerel
udang	prawn	*adik*	younger brother, younger sister

udang galah	lobster	*kakak*	elder sister
ketam	crab	*cucu*	grandchild
belut	eel	*datuk*	grandfather
ular	snake	*nenek*	grandmother

CONVERSATION FOUR
Around the house: Sickness

Mrs. Smith:	*Aminah, ada barang-barang di dalam kereta.* Aminah, there are some things in the car. *Tolong bawa masuk ke rumah.* Please bring them into the house. *Baik-baik jangan kasi pecah telur-telur itu.* Be careful not to break the eggs.
Aminah:	*Baiklah!* All right!
Mrs. Smith:	*Hari ini panas. Tolong buat sedikit teh.* It's hot today. Please make some tea.
Aminah:	*Hari nak hujan. Ada awan di langit.* It'll rain today. There are clouds in the sky. *Saya mahu cuci cadar, tapi saya takut hujan.* I wanted to wash the bedsheets, but I was afraid of rain.
Mrs. Smith:	*Awak sudah habis seterika baju kemeja tuan?* Have you finished ironing the master's shirts?
Aminah:	*Ia, sudah habis.* Yes, I've finished. *Tapi stoking-stoking tuan ada lubang.* But there are holes in his socks. *Stoking-stoking itu mesti dijerumat.* They need darning.
Mrs. Smith:	*Awak ada kanji baju kemeja tuan?* Did you starch the master's shirts?
Aminah:	*Tidak. Mem cakap tak usah.* No. You told me not to. *Apa saya mesti masak untuk makan tengahari?* What should I cook for lunch?

Mrs. Smith:	*Tolong kupas ubi kentang dan rebus sekali.*
	You can peel some potatoes and boil them.
	Tolong masakkan lobak itu.
	And prepare some carrots.
Aminah:	*Baiklah!*
	All right!
	Mem, mem di sebelah itu sakit pagi tadi.
	Madam, the lady next door is ill this morning.
	Doktor ada datang periksa.
	The doctor came to examine her.
Mrs. Smith:	*Oh, kena apa dia?*
	Oh, what's the matter with her?
Aminah:	*Amah dia cakap, dia ada sakit kepala, dan muntah-muntah.*
	Her amah says, she has a headache and has been vomiting.
	Doktor beri dia sedikit ubat.
	The doctor gave her some medicine.
Mrs. Smith:	*Dia tak pergi hospital?*
	She is not going to the hospital?
	Tak teruklah!
	It's not that serious.
Aminah:	*Saya sakit gigi malam tadi. Saya tak dapat tidur.*
	I had a toothache last night. I couldn't sleep.
Mrs. Smith:	*Awak mesti pergi jumpa doktor gigi.*
	You must go to the dentist.

Vocabulary:

barang	things	*masak*	cook
baik-baik	take care	*kupas*	peel
jaga baik-baik	—do—	*rebus*	boil
		sakit	ill
hujan	rain	*periksa*	investigate, enquire, examine
awan	cloud		
langit	sky		
cadar	bedsheet	*kena*	experience

takut	fearful, fear	*kena sakit*	to fall ill
seterika	iron, press	*kepala*	head; also used for headman, foreman
baju	jacket (in Malay clothes)	*muntah*	vomit
baju kemeja	shirt	*ubat*	medicine
habis	done, finished	*teruk*	severe (of illness)
		gigi	tooth
stoking	sock, stocking	*dapat*	get, obtain
		jumpa	encounter
lubang	hole	*doktor gigi*	dentist
jerumat	darning	*kanji*	starch
tak usah	needless		

Additional Vocabulary:

The following words may be useful:

bulan	moon	*selsema*	cold (in the head)
matahari	sun	*potong*	a cut; to operate
seluar	trousers	*lebam*	bruise
s. panjang	long trousers	*jururawat*	nurse
s. pendek	short trousers, shorts	*kain balut*	bandage
		minyak ubat	ointment
panjang	long		
pendek	short	*darah*	blood
demam	fever	*suhu*	temperature

CONVERSATION FIVE
In the Kitchen

Mrs. Smith:	*Tolong rebus ubi kentang itu.*
	Please boil these potatoes.
	Kemudian masak daging cincang ini di dalam kuali.
	Then cook these chops in the frying pan.
Aminah:	*Mem mahu makan halwa hari ini?*
	Are you having stewed fruit today?
	Boleh tak saya suruh orang beli aiskrim?
	Should I send someone for ice-cream?
Mrs. Smith:	*Ini hari kita makan buah-buahan.*
	Today we shall have fresh fruit.
	Tolong siapkan meja.
	Please set the table.
	Mahu garam dan lada putih.
	We want salt and pepper.
	Tak mahu sawi-sawi.
	We don't want mustard.
Aminah:	*Tuan minum bir tak?*
	Will master be drinking beer?
Mrs. Smith:	*Tidak.*
	No.
	Kita mesti cermat.
	We must save money.
	Tuan minum air.
	Master will drink water.
Aminah:	*Bir sudah tak ada, mem.*
	There's no beer left, ma'am.
	Mem minum satu botol pagi tadi.
	You drank a bottle this morning.

Mrs. Smith:	*Itu bukan bir.* That wasn't beer. *Itu lemonad. Minuman ringan.* That was lemonade. A soft drink. *Tolong tanya tukang kebun kalau buah betik itu sudah masak?* Will you ask the gardener if the papayas are ripe?
Aminah:	*Dia cakap, belum masak lagi.* He says they are not ripe yet. *Tapi ini sedikit pisang dari tukang kebun.* But here are some bananas from the gardener. *Dia tanya kalau mem mahu buah kelapa?* He asked if you would like some coconuts?
Mrs. Smith:	*Ia. Dia boleh bawa sedikit.* Yes. He can bring me a couple. *Yang lebih dia boleh simpan.* He can keep the rest for himself.
Aminah:	*Mem, peti ais itu sudah rosak.* Madam, there's something wrong with the ice-box. *Tak sejuk. Tak ada air batu.* It's not cold. There is no ice.
Mrs. Smith:	*Sudah buka suis?* Is it switched on?
Aminah:	*Ia, sudah buka.* Yes, it's switched on.
Mrs. Smith:	*Saya mesti telefon suruh tukang datang.* I must telephone for the men to come. *Mesti ada yang salah.* Something must be faulty.

Vocabulary:

kemudian	afterwards	*tukang*	skilled workman
kuali	a cooking pan	*tukang kebun*	gardener
siap	ready		

halwa	anything preserved in sugar	*masak*	ripe; to cook
		belum	not yet
		daripada	from
buah-buahan	fruits in general, fruit of all sorts	*yang lebih*	the most, the more, the rest
		simpan	keep, put away
siapkan	to get ready	*rosak*	spoilt, injured
lada putih	pepper	*air batu*	ice
sawi-sawi	mustard	*buka*	to open
cermat	economise	*buka suis*	to switch on
minuman ringan	a soft drink	*salah*	faulty, error
		tanya	ask, enquire

Additional Vocabulary:

The following words may be useful:

Bedroom		*House*	
bantal	pillow	*tingkap*	window
bantal peluk	bolster	*pintu*	door
tilam	mattress	*tangga*	staircase, ladder
katil	bed	*dinding*	partition
kelambu	mosquito net		

Parts of the body

rambut	hair	*dada*	chest
hidung	nose	*perut*	stomach
bibir	lips	*lengan*	arm
mulut	mouth	*siku*	elbow
dagu	chin	*jari*	finger
leher	neck	*kaki*	leg, foot
bahu	shoulder	*tulang*	bone

CONVERSATION SIX
The Perfect Car

Mrs. Smith: *George, kereta ini mesti ada yang rosak.*
George, there's something wrong with the car.

Mr. Smith: *Apa awak sudah buat?*
What have you done?

Mrs. Smith: *Saya tak buat apa-apa. Sterengnya tak betul, dan breknya tak makan.*
I've done nothing. The steering doesn't function properly, and the brake doesn't work.

Mr. Smith: *Baiklah. Saya hantar untuk dibaiki.*
All right. I'll take it to be repaired.
Saya hendak mereka baiki windscreen-wiper sekali.
I want them to repair the windscreen-wiper at the same time.

Mrs. Smith: *Pagi ini saya bawa kereta, tapi kereta lain himpit saya ke tepi. Saya langgar tiang lampu.*
I was driving this morning, but I was forced into the kerb by another car: I bumped into a lamp post.

Mr. Smith: *Saya fikir ada yang salah.*
I thought there was something wrong.
Apa yang rosak?
What's the damage?

Mrs. Smith: *Ada lekuk di mudguard depan, dan catnya calar.*
There's a dent in the front mudguard and the paint is scratched.
George kenapa awak tak betulkan pemegang pintu depan di sebelah kanan?

George, why don't you get the handle of the front right-hand door repaired?

Mr. Smith: *Saya akan betulkan sendiri bila saya ada masa.*
I shall mend it myself when I have time.
Saya tak tahu kenapa awak selalu berlanggar.
I don't know why you have all these accidents.

Mrs. Smith: *Bukan salah saya. Saya ambil nombor kereta itu. X 1234.*
It was not my fault. I took the number of the other car. X 1234.

Mr. Smith: *Saya mesti tulis surat kepada syarikat insuran.*
I must write to the insurance company.

Mrs. Smith: *Awak ada bayar wang insuran yang lepas?*
Did you pay the last premium?

Mr. Smith: *Ia. Sudah tentu. Saya fikir begitu. Boleh jadi.*
Yes. Of course. I think so. Perhaps.

Mrs. Smith: *Tayar itu kurang angin, dan yang belakang mesti ditukar.*
The tyres need air, and one at the back needs changing.
Bau asap dari ekzos masuk dalam kereta.
The smell from the exhaust comes into the car.

Mr. Smith: *Baiklah. Saya akan buat itu semua.*
All right. I'll see to it all.

Mrs. Smith: *George, kenapa kita tak beli kereta baharu?*
George, why don't we buy a new car?

Mr. Smith: *Kita tak mahu kereta baharu.*
We don't need a new car.
Kereta ini banyak bagus.
Our present car is a very good model.
Buatannya kuat dan bagus.
There's quality of workmanship in it.

Vocabulary:

betul	correct	*langgar*	knock against
hantar	convey, send	*fikir*	think

tak makan	doesn't work (a common colloquialism)	*lekuk*	hollow, puddle
		calar	a scratch
		tepi	edge, border

Additional Vocabulary:

sendiri	self, personally	*himpit*	wedge, squeeze
selalu	always, continually	*tiang*	post, pillar
		lampu	lamp
kepada	to	*depan*	front
lepas	past, ago, since	*cat*	paint
tentu	certain, definite	*kenapa*	why
		masa	time, season
sudah tentu	of course	*berlanggar*	accident
belakang	back, behind	*bayar*	pay
bau	smell	*wang*	money
asap	smoke	*begitu*	in that way, so
bila	when, whenever	*jadi*	become, coming into existence
betulkan	to repair	*boleh jadi*	perhaps, maybe
rosak	broken, injured, spoilt	*angin*	wind, air
		buatan	workmanship
kurang	less, lacking in	*kuat*	good, strong
kereta	car	*insuran*	insurance
syarikat	company		

CONVERSATION SEVEN
Things for the House

Mrs. Smith: *Saya mahu beli sedikit barang-barang untuk rumah.*
I want to buy some things for the house.
Awak mahu ikut tak?
Are you coming with me?

Mr. Smith: *Saya fikir baik saya ikut.*
I suppose I'll have to.
Awak mahu ke mana?
Where do you want to go?

Mrs. Smith: *Ada kedai-kedai di High Street.*
There are some shops in High Street.
Mula-mula saya mahu beli kuali.
I want to buy some pans first.

Mr. Smith: *Kita tak boleh letak kereta di High Street.*
We can't park the car in High Street.
Saya mesti pergi ke tempat letakereta.
I must go to the car park.

Mrs. Smith: *Kita masuk kedai ini dahulu.*
We'll go into this shop first.

(To shopkeeper)
Berapa harga kuali-kuali ini?
How much are these frying pans?

Shopkeeper: *Yang kecil dua ringgit. Yang besar lima ringgit.*
The small ones are two dollars. The big ones five dollars.
Ada banyak macam kuali dan barang-barang dapur.
We have a wide range of pans and things for the kitchen.

Mem mahu berus?
Do you want any brushes?
Berus baharu datang.
They've just come in.
Bagus punya berus, penyapu, berus sepatu.
Very good brushes, brooms, shoe brushes.

Mrs. Smith: *Saya juga mahu kain lap.*
I also want some dusters.
Beri saya satu tapisan.
(And) please give me a colander.

Shopkeeper: *Nanti saya bungkus semua dan hantar kepada mem.*
I'll wrap them all up and send them to you.
Mem duduk di mana?
What address?

(In the next shop)

Mrs. Smith: *Saya mahu cari kelambu.*
I want to see some mosquito nets.

Shopkeeper: *Untuk katil besar atau kecil?*
For a double bed or a single?

Mrs. Smith: *Untuk katil budak.*
For a child's bed.
Kita tak gunakan kelambu.
We don't use them.
Yang ini tak berapa bagus.
This one isn't very good.
Tunjuk saya yang lain.
Show me another.

Shopkeeper: *Ada apa-apa lagi mem mahu?*
Is there anything else you want.
Cadar? Sarung bantal? Ada tilam yang bagus.
Bedsheets? Pillow-cases? We have some very good mattresses.
Banyak lembut.
They are very soft.

Mrs. Smith:	*Tidak. Itu sahaja.* No. That's all. *Tolong bungkuskan kelambu itu.* Please wrap up the mosquito net. *George, tolong bayarkan. Saya mahu pergi kedai sebelah.* George, please pay for them. I want to go to the shop next door.

(In the next shop)

Mrs. Smith:	*Saya mahu tengok set teh.* I want to see some tea sets. *Ini buatan mana? Buatan Englandkah?* Where was this made? Was it made in England?
Shopkeeper:	*Bukan. Buatan Jepun. Banyak bagus.* No. It is Japanese. It's very good. *Ada set makan yang sama corak.* We have a dinner set with the same pattern. *Mem mahu tengok?* Would you like to see it?
Mrs. Smith:	*Saya fikir ini bagus.* I think this is very nice. *Boleh tolong hantar ke rumah saya?* Could you send it to my house?
Shopkeeper:	*Mem bayar tunai atau pun masuk dalam akaun?* Will you pay cash or should I enter it on account?
Mrs. Smith:	*Tolong hantar bil ke rumah saya.* Please send the bill to my house. *Hantar kepada Encik George Smith . . . .* Send it to Mr. George Smith . . . .

Vocabulary:

macam	sort, type	*ikut*	follow, go with
dapur	kitchen	*sarung*	
berus	brush	*bantal*	pillow cases
penyapu	broom	*lembut*	soft, tender

kain lap	duster	*keras*	hard
tapisan	colander	*contoh*	model
bungkus	wrap up	*tunai*	cash
guna	use	*pun*	(used for stress or for balance in the sentence)
gunakan	to make use of		
tunjuk	show, point out		
corak	pattern		

Additional Vocabulary:

seluar	pants, underpants	*sepatu*	shoe
		tali sepatu	shoe-laces
talileher (also *tie)*	tie	*tali*	string, rope
		jaket	jacket
seluar mandi	bathing trunks	*cawat*	suspenders
		baju mandi	swimsuit
mandi	to bathe	*topi*	hat
pakaian	frock, dress	*tudung*	scarf
baju	shirt	*sarung-tangan*	gloves
blaus	blouse		
skirt	skirt	*pipi*	cheeks
kain dalam	underskirt	*baju tidur*	nightdress, pyjamas
coli	brassiere	*seluar dalam*	panties

CONVERSATION EIGHT
A Few Repairs about the House

Aminah:	*Mem, ada enam buah kereta berhenti di depan rumah.*
	Madam, there are six cars stopping before the house.
Mrs. Smith:	*Cuba saya tengok.*
	Let me see.
	Alamak! Mereka datang serta-merta.
	Oh, no! They've all come at once.
	Bukakan pintu.
	Open the door.
1st Workman:	*Tukang elektrik, mem.*
	Electrician, ma'am.
Mrs. Smith:	*Loceng pintu tak boleh bunyi.*
	The door bell doesn't work.
	Ada dua suis lampu yang rosak.
	There are two light switches broken.
2nd Workman:	*Tukang gas mem. Adakah dapur gas yang mahu dibetulkan?*
	Gas, ma'am. Is it the gas stove that needs attention?
Mrs. Smith:	*Ia, tapi boleh jadi meternya pun rosak juga.*
	Yes, but there may be something wrong with the meter as well.
3rd Workman:	*Petisejuk, mem.*
	Fridge, ma'am.
	Saya mesti habiskan kerja saya semalam.
	I must finish the work I started yesterday.
4th Workman:	*Dia orang cakap bidai mahu dibetulkan.*
	They said the chicks need repairing.

Mrs. Smith: *Dua talinya putus.*
Two of the ropes are broken.
Aminah, tunjukkan dia di mana tali yang putus.
Aminah, show him where they are.

5th Workman: *Ada aduan fasal jamban tarik.*
There was a complaint about the lavatory cistern.

Mrs. Smith: *Ia. Dan paip air di atas sinki itu meleleh.*
Yes, and the tap on that sink is dripping.

5th Workman: *Boleh jadi kena tukar sesendal baharu.*
It probably needs a new washer.

6th Workman: *Kunci baharu untuk pintu depan dan belakang.*
New locks on front and back doors.
Dua daun tingkap sudah karat.
Shutters of two windows are rusty.

3rd Workman: *Mem, saya tak boleh uji petisejuk.*
Ma'am, I can't test the refrigerator.
Tak ada karen.
There's no electricity.

1st Workman: *Saya tak boleh buka suis pada masa saya betulkan.*
I can't switch it on while I'm repairing it.

2nd Workman: *Awak tak boleh gunakan blow-lamp itu sekarang. Ada gas di sekeliling.*
You can't use that blow lamp now. There's gas around.

5th Workman: *Mem mahu cuba jamban tarik sekarang?*
Would you like to try the lavatory now, ma'am?

Mrs. Smith: *Tidak.*
No.
Aminah, buatkan air teh.
Aminah, make some tea.
Ini terlalu banyak.
This is too much.

Aminah:	*Tak boleh mem. Tak ada gas.* I can't ma'am. There's no gas. *Mem pergi keluar tak?* Are you going out, ma'am?
Mrs. Smith:	*Ia. Saya mahu pergi tengok wayang gambar.* Yes. I am going to the cinema.

Vocabulary:

Alamak!	Good heavens!	*paip air*	water tap
sama	same	*meleleh*	drip, trickle
loceng	bell	*tukar*	change, substitute
bunyi	sound	*kunci*	lock
bidai	chicks, jalousies	*daun tingkap*	shutter
putus	broken (severed)		
aduan	complaint	*daun*	leaf
fasal	concerning	*karat*	rusty
jamban	W.C.	*karen*	electric current
tarik	pull, drag	*sekeliling*	position around
terlalu	surpassing, very		

Vocabulary:

Miscellaneous

gunting	scissors	*buang*	throw away
pasar	market	*sampah*	rubbish
penjual	salesman	*mati*	dead
kain	cloth	*bising*	loud noise, unpleasant noise
jarum	needle		
jahit	sew	*basuh*	wash
tikus	rat, mouse	*panggil*	call, summon, send for
turun	descend		
sorong	push	*basah*	wet
bohong	tell a lie, falsehood	*kering*	dry
		jatuh	fall, slip down

CONVERSATION NINE
Going on Holiday

Mary:	*Cuti sekolah mula hari esok.*
	The school holidays start tomorrow.
Mrs. Smith:	*Apa engkau hendak buat?*
	What are you going to do?
Mary:	*Saya mahu pergi makan angin dengan kereta.*
	I want to go travelling by car.
John:	*Saya mahu pergi ke negeri lain di masa cuti.*
	I should like to go away for my holidays.
Mary:	*Ke mana?*
	Where to?
John:	*Saya mahu pergi ke negeri India dengan kapal kecil.*
	I'd like to go to India in a small ship.
	Kapal layar.
	A sailing ship.
Mary:	*Itu bodoh. Itu makan masa yang lama.*
	That's silly. It would take too long.
	Saya mahu pergi ke Amerika dengan kapal-terbang.
	I'd like to to go America by aeroplane.
John:	*Awak mahu pergi ke Hollywood.*
	You only want to go to Hollywood.
	Saya mahu pergi ke Amerika Selatan, India, Masir dan lain-lain tempat.
	I want to go to South America, India, Egypt and all sorts of places.
Mary:	*Awak hendak pergi ke semua tempat itu?*
	You want to go to all these places?

	Saya fikir ada lebih baik pergi ke Amerika dan jadi seorang bintang filem.
	I think it's much better to go to America and be a film star.
John:	*Bukan tiap-tiap orang di Amerika itu bintang filem.*
	Not everyone in America is a film star.
Mary:	*Saya akan jadi.*
	I should be.
Mrs. Smith:	*Mari pergi makan angin dengan kapalterbang sekarang.*
	Let's go travelling by aeroplane now.
Mary:	*Ada pokok-pokok, dan rumput, dan bunga-bunga.*
	There are trees and grass and flowers.
	Ada burung-burung, dan binatang, dan nyamuk.
	There are birds, and animals and mosquitoes.
John:	*Kenapa awak cakap begitu?*
	Why are you saying that?
Mary:	*Saya hitung semua barang yang saya tengok.*
	I'm counting everything I can see.
	Orang-orang yang baca buku ini mahu belajar perkataan baharu.
	The people who are reading this book want to learn some new words.
John:	*Ada pejabat pos.*
	There's a post office.
	Setem, sampulsurat, surat-surat, pos kad, telegram, telefon.
	Stamps, envelopes, letters, post cards, telegram, telephone.
Mary:	*Tak mahu telefon.*
	We don't want telephone.
	Kita sudah ada di pelajaran yang dahulu.
	We had it in an earlier lesson.
Mrs. Smith:	*Engkau budak-budak cakap fasal apa?*
	What are you children talking about?

Mary:	*Kasihan emak, dia tak tahu fasal.* Poor mother, she doesn't know.

Vocabulary:

cuti	leave of absence, holiday	*dengan*	with
		tempat	place
mula	start	*kapal*	ship, boat
hendak	want, intend	*layar*	sail
jalan	go, walk; street	*bodoh*	silly, stupid
negeri	state, country	*terbang*	fly,flying
selatan	south	*kapal-terbang*	aeroplane
campur	mix, mingle		
bintang	a star, heavenly body	*perkataan*	word
		sarung	a sheath, something which wraps around
pokok	tree		
rumput	grass		
burung	bird	*kain sarung*	a sarong
binatang	animal	*surat*	letter
nyamuk	mosquito	*sampulsurat*	envelope
hitung	calculate, count	*pelajaran*	lesson, the thing taught
belajar	learn		
kasihan	pity	*emak*	mother

Additional Vocabulary:

masam	sour	*susah*	difficult, uneasy
cabai	chilli,	*lekas*	quick
	red pepper	*lambat*	slow
mangkuk	bowl	*tutup*	close
penuh	full	*hutan*	jungle
kosong	empty	*utara*	north
hijau	green	*timur*	east
pulau	island	*barat*	west
payung	umbrella	*bapa*	father
senang	comfortable, easy	*laut*	sea
		sungai	river

CONVERSATION TEN
An Evening Out

Note: *This conversation is written in the kind of Malay spoken among the Malays themselves. It contains many points of grammar not explained in this course.*

Aminah: *Selamat pagi, Mat.*
Good morning, Ahmad.
Awak dah baca suratkhabar pagi ini belum?
Have you seen the newspaper this morning?

Ahmad: *Belum. Ada berita apa?*
Not yet. What's the news?

Aminah: *Katanya dalam suratkhabar, kalau kita hendak mendaftarkan nama untuk pilihanraya, kita mesti berbuat demikian sebelum penghujung minggu ini.*
It says in the paper that if we want to vote, we must register before the end of this week.
Dan ada juga berita air bah di negeri China.
And there have been floods in China.

Ahmad: *Apa ada air bah di negeri China kena-mengena dengan pilihanraya?*
What have floods in China got to do with voting?

Aminah: *Beritanya disiarkan di dalam mukasurat yang sama.*
They are on the same page in the newspaper.

Ahmad: *Awak hendak undi parti yang mana?*
What party are you going to vote for?

Aminah: *Saya tak boleh beritahu awak.*
I musn't tell you.
Undi mesti dirahsiakan.
Voting is to be secret.

Ahmad: *Baiklah.*
All right.
Kalau begitu saya tak mahu ajak awak pergi ke Great World malam ini.
Then I won't take you to the Great World tonight.

Aminah: *Saya tak ada cakap yang saya nak ikut awak.*
I never said I'd go with you.
Omar pun dah ajak saya pergi.
Omar has asked me as well.

Ahmad: *Saya tak pergi ke Great World malam ini.*
I'm not going to the Great World tonight.

Aminah: *Tetapi awak kata tadi awak nak pergi.*
But you just said you were.

Ahmad: *Saya sudah tukar fikiran saya.*
I've changed my mind.
Saya nak tengok wayang gambar.
I'm going to the cinema instead.
Awak hendak ikut tengok wayang gambar tak?
Would you like to come to the cinema?

Aminah: *Mengapa awak tak mahu ikut Omar dan saya ke Great World?*
Why don't you come to the Great World with Omar and me?

Ahmad: *Kalau berdua genap, tetapi bertiga ganjil.*
Two's company, three's not.

Aminah: *Awak cemburu dengan Omar.*
You're jealous of Omar.

Ahmad: *Tidak. Saya tak cemburu.*
No. I'm not.
Awak boleh pergi ke Great World bersama-sama Omar.
You can go to the Great World with Omar.
Saya hendak melihat wayang gambar.
I'm going to the cinema.

Aminah: *Sudah tentu awak tak suka melihat wayang seorang diri.*

	You won't like it by yourself.
Ahmad:	*Saya tak pergi bersendirian.*
	I'm not going by myself.
	Saya akan pergi bersama-sama Asiah.
	I am going with Asiah.
Aminah:	*Tetapi saya fikir awak nak ajak saya.*
	But I thought you were taking me.
Ahmad:	*Awak tak mahu ikut.*
	You didn't want to come.
Aminah:	*Tidak, saya mahu.*
	Yes, I do.

VOCABULARY

Each word has been given a letter and a number. The Letter 'L' means that the number refers to one of the Lessons in Part One of the book. For example, a word marked L3 would be found in Lesson Three. A word marked C3 would be found in Conversation Three.

The purpose of this index is not only to enable the reader to find the translation of the required word, but also to note how it is used when it is first introduced. The numbers refer only to the first appearance of the words in the text of the book, and not to any subsequent appearance.

English/Malay

able	*boleh*	L 6
accident	*berlanggar*	C 6
aeroplane	*kapal-terbang*	C 9
afternoon, early	*tengahari*	L 6
late	*petang*	L 6
afterwards	*kemudian*	C 5
age	*umur*	L 8
air	*angin*	C 6
all	*semua*	C 1
all right	*baik*	L 4
all the same	*juga*	C 1
also	*juga*	C 7
always	*selalu*	C 6
ancient	*lama*	L 8
and	*dan*	L 2
animal	*binatang*	C 9
another	*lain*	L 8
anybody	*siapa-siapa*	C 1
anything	*lain-lain*	C 1
anywhere	*mana-mana*	L10
arm	*lengan*	C 5
ask	*tanya*	C 5
at	*pada*	L 9
back	*belakang*	C 6
ball	*bola*	L 3
banana	*pisang*	L 5
bandage	*kain balut*	C 4
bank	*batas*	C 2
bar (of a cage)	*bilah*	L 5

basket	*bakul*	L 6
bath, bathe	*mandi*	C 7
bathing trunks	*seluar mandi*	C 7
beans	*kacang*	C 2
long beans	*kacang panjang*	
sword beans	*kacang parang*	
french beans	*kacang boncis*	
bean sprouts	*taugih*	C 2
become	*jadi*	C 6
bed	*katil*	C 5
bedroom	*bilik tidur*	L 6
bedsheet	*cadar*	C 4
before	*dahulu*	L 4
behind	*di balik*	L10
bell	*loceng*	C 8
big	*besar*	L 1
bird	*burung*	C 9
bitter	*pahit*	C 1
black	*hitam*	L 2
blood	*darah*	C 4
blotting paper	*kertas tekap*	C 1
blouse	*blaus*	C 7
blue	*biru*	L 1
blue-black	*biru tua*	C 1
boil	*rebus*	C 4
bolster	*bantal peluk*	C 5
bone	*tulang*	C 5
book	*buku*	L 8
border	*tepi*	C 6
bottle	*botol*	C 1
bowl	*mangkuk*	C 9
boy, young	*budak*	L 6
brand	*cap*	C 1
brassiere	*coli*	C 7
bread	*roti*	L 5
bring	*bawa, ambilkan,*	L 8
brinjals	*terung*	C 2
broken	*rosak,*	C 6
	putus	C 8
	pecah	L 5
broom	*penyapu*	C 7
brother, elder	*abang*	C 3
younger	*adik*	C 3
bruise	*lebam*	C 4
brush	*berus*	C 7
but	*tapi*	L 4
butter	*mentega*	C 3
buy	*beli*	L 5
by	*pada*	L 9

cabbage	*kobis*	C 2
calculate	*hitung*	C 9
call	*panggil*	C 8
car	*kereta*	C 6
careful	*baik-baik*	C 4
carrot	*lobak merah*	C 2
cash	*tunai*	C 7
cat fish	*ikan sembilang*	C 3
cent	*sen*	L 3
certain	*tentu*	C 6
chair	*kerusi*	L 1

change	*tukar*	C 8
cheap	*murah*	C 2
cheeks	*pipi*	C 7
chest	*kotak*	L 9
chest (body)	*dada*	C 5
chicken	*ayam*	C 3
chicks	*bidai*	C 8
child	*kanak-kanak*	L 3
chili	*cabai*	C 9
chin	*dagu*	C 5
chocolate	*coklat*	C 1
chop (pork)	*babi cincang*	C 3
cigarette	*rokok*	L 5
clean	*bersih*	L 1
clock	*jam*	L 7
close	*tutup*	C 9
cloth	*kain*	C 8
cloud	*awan*	C 4
coconut	*kelapa*	C 5
coco-yam	*keladi*	C 2
coffee	*air kopi*	L 4
colander	*tapisan*	C 7
cold	*sejuk*	L 4
cold (illness)	*selsema*	C 4
come	*datang*	L 7
come here	*mari*	L 4
come in	*masuk*	L 8
comfortable	*senang*	C 9
companion	*kawan*	C 2
complaint	*aduan*	C 8
complete	*genap*	C10
concerning	*fasal*	C 8
container	*kotak*	L 9
content	*isi*	C 3
convey	*hantar*	C 6
cook	*masak*	C 4
cooking oil	*minyak makan*	C 3
cooking pan	*kuali*	C 5
coolie lines	*bangsal*	C 2
correct	*betul*	C 6
costly	*mahal*	C 1
country	*negeri*	C 9
crab	*ketam*	C 3
cracked	*retak*	L 5
cucumber	*timun*	C 2
cup	*cawan*	L 1
cupboard	*almari*	L 8
cut, a	*cincang*	C 3
cut off, to	*potong*	C 3
cutting	*cincang*	C 3
darning	*jerumat*	C 4
day	*hari*	L 3
dead	*mati*	C 8
dear	*mahal*	C 1
dent	*lubang*	C 4
dentist	*doktor gigi*	C 4
descend	*turun*	C 8
diary	*buku peringatan*	C 1
difficult	*susah*	C 9
dinner	*makan-malam*	L 7
dirty	*kotor*	L 1
do	*buat*	L 6
do not	*jangan*	L 9
does not work	*tak makan*	C 6

dog	*anjing*	L 6
dog fish	*ikan yu*	C 3
dollar	*ringgit*	L 2
done	*sudah habis*	L 7
	dah	C10
door	*pintu*	C 5
drag	*tarik*	C 8
dress	*pakaian*	C 7
drink	*minum*	L 4
drink, soft	*minuman ringan*	C 5
drip	*meleleh*	C 8
duck	*itik*	C 3
duster	*kain lap*	C 7
dwell	*duduk*	L 6
early afternoon	*tengahari*	L 6
east	*timur*	C 9
eat	*makan*	L 3
economise	*cermat*	C 5
edge	*tepi*	C 6
eel	*belut*	C 3
egg	*telur*	L 3
eight	*lapan*	L 3
elbow	*siku*	C 5
elder brother	*abang*	C 3
elder sister	*kakak*	C 3
election	*pilihanraya*	C10
electric current	*karen*	C 8
eleven	*sebelas*	L 3
empty	*kosong*	C 9
encounter	*jumpa*	C 4
end	*hujung*	C10
enquire	*tanya,*	C 5
	periksa	C 4
envelope	*sampul-surat*	C 9
error	*salah*	C 5
European	*orang putih*	C 2
even	*genap*	C10
evening	*petang*	L 6
ever	*pernah*	C 2
every	*tiap-tiap*	L 7
every day	*hari-hari*	L 3
everything	*semua*	C 1
examine	*periksa*	C 4
extinguish	*padam*	C 1
eye	*mata*	L 9
face	*muka*	L 9
fall	*jatuh*	C 8
fall ill	*kena sakit*	C 4
falsehood	*bohong*	C 8
fat	*lemak, minyak*	C 3
father	*bapa*	C 9
fault	*salah*	C 5
fear	*takut*	C 4
fearful	*takut*	C 4
female	*perem-puan*	L 3
fever	*demam*	C 4
fifteen	*lima belas*	L 3
filling	*isi*	C 3
fine	*elok*	L 2
fine (good)	*bagus*	C 2
finger	*jari*	C 5
finished	*sudah,*	L 7
	habis	C 4

first	*dahulu*	L 4
firstly	*mula-mula*	L 4
fish	*ikan*	C 3
five	*lima*	L 2
flavour	*rasa*	C 2
floods	*air bah*	C10
floor	*lantai*	L 1
flower	*bunga*	L 5
fly, to	*terbang*	C 9
flying	*terbang*	C 9
follow	*ikut*	C 7
foot	*kaki*	C 5
for	*untuk*	C 1
foreman	*kepala*	C 4
forget	*lupa*	L 9
fork	*garpu*	L 5
four	*empat*	L 2
french beans	*kacang boncis*	C 2
Friday	*hari lima, Jumaat*	L10
friend	*kawan*	C 2
frock	*pakaian*	C 7
from	*daripada, dari*	C 5 L10
front	*depan*	C 6
fruit	*buah*	L 2
fruit (in general)	*buah-buahan*	C 5
fry	*goreng*	L 6
full	*penuh*	C 9
garden	*kebun*	L 4
gardener	*tukang kebun*	C 5
get	*dapat*	C 4

girl, young	*perempuan*	L 6
give	*kasi*	L 2
glasses	*cermin-mata*	L 9
gloves	*sarung-tangan*	C 7
go	*pergi*	L 4
go out	*keluar*	L 7
go shopping	*pergi kedai*	C 1
go up	*naik*	C 9
goat	*kambing*	L 7
good (fine)	*bagus*	C 2
good (strong)	*kuat*	C 6
good (tasty)	*sedap*	L 4
good	*baik*	L 4
good heavens	*Alamak*	C 8
good morning	*pagi*	C 1
goose	*angsa*	C 3
grain	*biji*	L 2
grandchild	*cucu*	C 3
grandfather	*datuk*	C 3
grandmother	*nenek*	C 3
grass	*rumput*	C 9
grease	*lemak*	C 3
green	*hijau*	C 9
hair	*rambut*	C 5
half	*setengah*	L 7
handkerchief	*sapu-tangan*	L 9
hanging	*gantung*	L 7
hard	*keras*	C 7
hat	*topi*	C 7

have	*ada*	L 2
he	*dia*	L 3
head	*kepala*	C 4
headman	*ketua*	C 4
help	*tolong*	L 7
here	*sini*	L 4
hole	*lubang*	C 4
holiday	*cuti*	C 9
hollow	*lekuk*	C 6
honey	*madu*	C 3
hot	*panas*	L 4
hour	*jam*	L 7
house	*rumah*	L 1
how many	*berapa, berapa banyak*	L 2
how much	*berapa, berapa banyak, berapa harga*	L 2
hundred	*ratus*	L 3
husband	*suami*	L 3
I	*saya*	L 1
ice	*air batu*	C 5
if	*kalau*	C 1
ill	*sakit*	C 4
ill, to fall	*kena sakit*	C 4
in	*di dalam*	L 6
india rubber	*getah padam*	C 1
injured	*rosak*	C 6
ink	*dakwat*	C 1
intent	*hendak*	C 9
investigate	*periksa*	C 4
invite	*ajak*	C10
iron	*seterika*	C 4
is it that	*adakah*	L 2
island	*pulau*	C 9
jacket (Malay)	*baju*	C 4
jacket (European)	*jaket*	C 7
jack fruit	*nangka*	C 2
jalousies	*bidai*	C 8
jealous	*cemburu*	C10
jungle	*hutan*	C 9
keep	*simpan*	C 5
kilogramme	*kilogram*	L 2
kitchen	*dapur*	C 7
knife	*pisau*	L 5
knock against	*langgar*	C 6
know	*tahu*	L 7
ladder	*tangga*	C 5
ladies fingers	*kacang bendi*	C 2
lamp	*lampu*	C 6
lard	*minyak babi*	C 3
late afternoon	*petang*	L 6
latex	*susu getah*	C 2
leaf	*daun*	C 8
learn	*belajar*	C 9
leave	*cuti*	C 9
left	*kiri*	L 8
leg	*kaki*	C 5

lemon	*limau*	C 2
less	*kurang*	C 6
lesson	*pelajaran*	C 9
letter	*surat*	C 9
lie	*bohong*	C 8
like	*suka*	L 3
lime	*limau*	C 2
line	*satar*	C 1
lips	*bibir*	C 5
little	*sedikit*	L 9
live	*duduk*	L 6
lobster	*udang galah*	C 3
lock	*kunci*	C 8
locker	*kotak*	L 9
long	*panjang*	C 4
long (of time)	*lama*	L 8
long beans	*kacang panjang*	C 2
long pepper	*cabai*	C 9
look at	*tengok*	L 9
look for	*cari*	L 9
lose	*rugi*	C 1
loud	*bising*	C 8

mackerel	*ikan tenggiri*	C 3
madam	**see Lesson Five**	
male	*laki-laki*	L 3
man	*orang laki-laki*	L 3
mango	*mangga*	C 2
mangosteen	*manggis*	C 2
manner	*gaya*	L 8
many	*banyak*	L 2
many (how?)	*berapa*	L 2
market	*pasar*	C 8
master	*tuan*	L 5
mattress	*tilam*	C 5
may be	*boleh jadi*	C 6
me	*saya*	L 1
meat	*daging*	L 2
medicine	*ubat*	C 4
midday	*tengahari*	L 6
middle	*tengah*	
milk	*susu*	L 4
mingle	*campur*	C 9
mirror	*cermin*	L 9
mix	*campur*	C 9
model	*contoh*	C 7
Monday	*hari satu, Isnin*	L10
money	*duit,*	L 5
	wang	C 6
month	*bulan*	L 6
moon	*bulan*	C 4
more	*lagi,*	C 1
	lebih	L10
more or less	*lebih kurang*	L10
morning	*pagi*	L 6
mosquito	*nyamuk*	C 9
mosquito net	*kelambu*	C 5
mother	*emak*	C 9
mount, to	*naik*	L 9
mouse	*tikus*	C 8
mouth	*mulut*	C 5
Mr., Mrs.	**see Lesson Five**	
much	*banyak*	L 2

much (how?)	*berapa banyak*	L 2
museum	*sekolah gambar*	L10
must	*mesti*	L 7
mustard	*sawi-sawi*	C 5
my	*saya*	L 1
name	*nama*	L 9
near	*pada*	L 9
neck	*leher*	C 5
needle	*jarum*	C 8
needless	*tak usah*	C 4
never	*tak pernah*	C 2
newspaper	*surat-khabar*	C 1
next door	*di sebelah*	C 3
nib	*mata pen*	C 1
night	*malam*	L 6
nightdress	*baju tidur*	C 7
nine	*sembilan*	L 3
no	*tidak, tak*	L 1
no (contradicting)	*bukan*	C 1
noise	*bising*	C 8
north	*utara*	C 9
nose	*hidung*	C 5
not	*tidak*	L 1
not yet	*belum*	C 5
now	*sekarang*	C 1
nurse	*jururawat*	C 4
obtain	*dapat*	C 4
occasion	*kali*	C 1
o'clock	*pukul*	L 7
of course	*sudah tentu*	C 6
offspring	*anak*	L 3
oil	*minyak*	C 3
oil, cooking	*minyak makan*	C 3
ointment	*minyak ubat*	C 4
old	*tua, lama*	L 8
on	*di atas*	L 6
once	*sekali*	C 1
one	*satu, se*	L 2
only	*sahaja*	C 1
open	*buka*	C 5
operate (surgical)	*potong*	C 4
or	*atau*	C 3
orange	*limau*	C 2
other	*lain*	L 8
own	*punya*	L 9
ox	*lembu*	L 7
packet	*kotak*	L 9
paddy field	*sawah*	C 2
page	*muka*	C10
paint	*cat*	C 6
pan, cooking	*kuali*	C 5
panties	*seluar dalam*	C 7
pants	*seluar*	C 7
papaya	*buah betik*	L 4
paper	*kertas*	C 1
paper, blotting	*kertas tekap*	C 1
partition	*dinding*	C 5
party	*pihak*	C10
past	*lepas*	C 6
pattern	*contoh*	C 7

pay	*bayar*	C 6
pearl	*mutiara*	C 3
peel	*kupas*	C 4
people	*orang*	L 3
pepper	*lada*	C 5
pepper, long	*cabai*	C 9
pepper, white	*lada putih*	C 5
perhaps	*kadang-kadang,*	L 6
	boleh jadi	C 6
picture	*gambar*	L 9
pictures	*wayang gambar*	L 9
pig	*babi*	L 7
pillar	*tiang*	C 6
pillow	*bantal*	C 5
pillowcase	*sarung bantal*	C 7
pineapples	*buah nenas*	L 2
pity	*kasihan*	C 9
place	*tempat*	C 9
plate	*pinggan*	L 1
play	*main*	L 3
please (when giving an instruction)	*tolong*	L 7
please	*sila*	L 8
point	*hujung*	C10
point out	*tunjuk*	C 7
policeman	*mata-mata*	L 9
pork chop	*babi cincang*	C 3
position around	*sekeliling*	C 8
post	*tiang*	C 8

potato	*ubi kentang*	L 5
potato, sweet	*keledek*	C 2
powder (cosmetic)	*bedak*	L 9
powder compact	*kotak bedak*	L 9
prawn	*udang*	C 3
preserves	*halwa*	C 5
press	*seterika*	C 4
pretty	*cantik*	L 2
price	*harga*	L 2
price, what	*berapa harga*	L 2
proper	*patut*	C 2
pull	*tarik*	C 8
push	*sorong*	C 8
put	*taruh*	L10
put away	*simpan*	C 5
pyjamas	*baju tidur*	C 7
quarter (¼)	*suku*	L 7
quick	*lekas*	C 9
radish	*lobak putih*	C 2
rain	*hujan*	C 4
rat	*tikus*	C 8
read	*baca*	L 8
ready	*siap*	C 5
ready, to get	*siapkan*	C 5
receive	*terima*	C 1
recently	*tadi*	L 9
red	*merah*	L 1
reduce	*kurangkan*	C 6

register	*mendaftar*	C10
repair, to	*betulkan*	C 6
return	*balik*	L 9
rice, cooked	*nasi*	C 2
rice, uncooked	*beras*	C 2
rice, unhusked	*padi*	C 2
ridge	*batas*	C 2
right (direction)	*kanan*	L 8
right	*patut*	C 2
ripe	*masak*	C 5
river	*sungai*	C 9
rod	*batang*	L 5
room	*bilik*	L 1
rouge	*gincu pipi*	C 7
rubber	*getah*	C 1
rubber estate	*kebun getah*	C 2
rubber, india	*getah padam*	C 1
rubber tapping	*toreh getah*	C 2
rubber tree	*pokok getah*	C 2
rubbish	*sampah*	C 8
ruler	*kayu satar*	C 1
rusty	*karat*	
sail	*layar*	C 9
salesman	*penjual*	C 8
salt	*garam*	L 5
same	*sama*	C 8
sarong	*kain sarung*	C 9
Saturday	*hari Sabtu*	L10
saucer	*piring*	L 1
saying	*kata*	C10
scarf	*tudung*	C 7
school	*sekolah*	L 1
scissors	*gunting*	C 8
scratch, a	*calar*	C 6
sea	*laut*	C 9
see	*nampak,*	L 9
	tengok	L 9
seed	*biji*	L 2
self	*sendiri*	C 6
sell	*jual*	L 5
send	*hantar*	C 6
send for	*panggil*	C 8
seven	*tujuh*	L 3
severe	*teruk*	C 4
severed	*putus*	C 8
sew	*jahit*	C 8
shall	*akan*	L 8
shark	*ikan yu*	C 3
she	*dia*	L 3
sheath, a	*sarung*	C 9
shed	*bangsal*	C 2
sheep	*kambing*	L 7
ship	*kapal*	C 9
smoke	*asap*	C 6
shirt	*baju kemeja*	C 4
shoe(s)	*sepatu*	C 7
shoelaces	*tali sepatu*	C 7
shop	*kedai*	C 1

shopping, to go	*pergi kedai*	C 1
short	*pendek*	C 4
shorts	*seluar pendek*	C 4
shoulder	*bahu*	C 5
show	*tunjuk*	C 7
shutter	*daun tingkap*	C 8
sickle	*sabit*	C 2
side	*sebelah*	C 3
silly	*bodoh*	C 9
since	*lepas*	C 6
Singapore	*Singapura*	L 6
sister, elder	*kakak*	C 3
younger	*adik*	C 3
sit	*duduk*	L 6
six	*enam*	L 3
skilled workman	*tukang*	C 5
skirt (under-)	*kain dalam*	C 7
sky	*langit*	C 4
slashing	*cincang*	C 3
sleep	*tidur*	L 5
slip down	*jatuh*	C 8
slow	*lambat*	C 9
small	*kecil*	L 1
	sedikit	L 9
smashed	*pecah*	L 5
smell	*bau*	C 6
smoke, to	*hisap rokok*	L 5
snake	*ular*	C 3
so	*begitu*	C 6
soap	*sabun*	L 4
sock	*stoking*	C 4
soft	*lembut*	C 7
soft drink	*minuman ringan*	C 5
sometimes	*kadang-kadang*	L 6
sort	*macam*	C 7
sound	*bunyi*	C 8
sour	*masam*	C 9
south	*selatan*	C 9
speak	*cakap*	L 8
spinach	*bayam*	C 2
spoilt	*rosak*	C 6
spoon	*sudu*	L 5
staircase	*tangga*	C 5
stand up	*bangun*	L 8
star	*bintang*	C 9
starch	*kanji*	C 4
start	*mula*	C 9
state	*negeri*	C 9
still	*juga*	C 1
sting ray	*ikan pari*	C 3
stocking	*stoking*	C 4
stomach	*perut*	C 5
stop	*berhenti*	L 8
street	*jalan*	C 9
strike	*pukul*	L 7
string	*tali*	C 7
strong	*kuat*	C 6
stupid	*bodoh*	C 9
substitute	*tukar*	C 8
sugar	*gula*	L 5
summon	*panggil*	C 8
sun	*matahari*	C 4
Sunday	*hari Minggu*	L10
supposing	*kalau*	C 1

sun glasses	*cerminmata hitam*	L10
surpassing	*terlalu*	C 8
suspended	*gantung*	L 7
suspenders	*cawat*	C 7
sweet	*manis*	C 1
sweet, a	*gula-gula*	C 1
sweet potato	*keledek*	C 2
swimsuit	*baju mandi*	C 7
switch on	*buka suis*	C 5
sword beans	*kacang parang*	C 2
table	*meja*	L 1
tail	*ekor*	L 5
take away	*ambil*	L 8
take care	*jaga baik-baik*	C 4
tapioca	*ubi kayu*	C 2
taste	*rasa*	C 2
tasty	*sedap*	L 4
tea	*air teh*	L 4
teacher	*guru*	L 8
-teen	*belas*	L 3
tell	*suruh*	L 3
temperature	*suhu*	C 4
ten	*sepuluh*	L 3
tender	*lembut*	C 7
thank you	*terimakasih*	C 1
that	*itu*	L 1
that one	*yang itu*	L 5
theatrical performance	*wayang*	L 9
there	*sana*	L 8
there is	*ada*	L 2
these	*ini*	L 1
they	*dia orang*	L 3
thick	*tebal*	C 3
thin	*tipis*	C 3
things	*barang*	C 4
think	*fikir*	C 6
this	*ini*	L 1
this one	*yang ini*	L 5
those	*itu*	L 1
thousand	*ribu*	L 9
three	*tiga*	L 2
throw away	*buang*	C 8
Thursday	*hari Khamis*	L10
tie	*talileher*	C 7
time	*kali,*	C 1
	masa	C 6
to	*kepada*	C 6
today	*hari ini*	L 6
tomorrow	*esok*	L 6
tone	*gaya*	L 8
tooth	*gigi*	C 4
tortoise	*kura-kura*	C 3
tree	*pokok*	C 9
trickle	*meleleh*	C 8
trousers	*seluar*	
long	*seluar panjang*	
short	*seluar pendek*	C 4
try	*cuba*	C 2
Tuesday	*hari Selasa*	L10
turkey	*ayam belanda*	C 3
turn	*belok*	L 8
turnip	*sengkuang*	C 2

turtle	*penyu*	C 3
twelve	*dua belas*	L 3
twenty	*dua puluh*	L 3
two	*dua*	L 2
type	*macam*	C 7
umbrella	*payung*	C 9
under	*bawah*	L 9
underskirt	*kain dalam*	C 7
uneasy	*susah*	C 9
uneven	*ganjil*	C10
urge	*ajak*	C10
use	*pakai*	L 9
use, make	*gunakan*	C 7
utterance	*kata*	C10
very	*terlalu*	C 8
vomit	*muntah*	C 4
vote	*undi*	C10
wait	*nanti*	L 4
walk	*jalan*	C 9
want	*hendak*	C 9
want, to	*mahu*	L 4
wash	*basuh,*	C 8
	cuci	L 4
wash clothes	*cuci kain*	L 4
wash dishes	*cuci pinggan*	L 4
water	*air*	L 4
water melon	*semangka*	C 2
water tap	*paip air*	C 8
W.C.	*jamban*	C 8
we	*kita*	L 5
wedge	*himpit*	C 6

Wednesday	*hari tiga, hari Rabu*	L10
week	*minggu*	L 6
west	*barat*	C 9
wet	*basah*	C 8
what	*apa*	L 2
whatever	*apa-apa*	C 3
what price	*berapa harga*	L 2
when	*bila*	C 6
whenever	*bila-bila*	C 6
where	*di mana*	L 6
where to	*ke mana*	L 9
white	*putih*	L 1
white pepper	*lada putih*	C 5
who	*siapa*	C 1
whole of, the	*semua*	C 1
why	*kenapa*	C 6
wife	*isteri*	C 2
wind	*angin*	C 6
window	*tingkap*	C 5
wish	*mahu*	L 4
with	*dengan*	C 9
woman	*orang perem-puan*	L 3
wood	*kayu*	C 1
word	*perkataan*	C 9
work	*kerja*	L 7
worker, skilled	*tukang*	C 5
workman-ship	*buatan*	C 6
wrap up	*bungkus*	C 7
write	*tulis*	L 8

year	*tahun*	L 6
yellow	*kuning*	L 5
yes	*ia*	L 2
yesterday	*semalam*	L 6
you	**see Lesson Five**	
young	*muda*	L 8

Malay/English

abang	elder brother	C 3
ada	have, there is, there are	L 2
adakah	is it that?	L 2
adik	younger brother	C 3
aduan	complaint	C 8
ajak	invite, urge	C10
akan	shall (intention)	L 8
Alamak	good heavens	C 8
almari	cupboard	L 8
ambilkan	bring	L 8
anak	child	L 3
angin	air, wind	C 6
angsa	goose	C 3
anjing	dog	L 6
apa	what	L 2
apa-apa	whatever	C 3
asap	smoke	C 6
atau	or	C 3
awak	you, person, self	L 3
awan	cloud	C 4
ayam	chicken	C 3
ayam belanda	turkey	C 3
air	water	L 4
air bah	floods	C10
air batu	ice	C 5

air kopi	coffee	L 4
air susu	milk	L 4
air teh	tea	L 4
babi	pig	L 7
babi cincang	pork chop	C 3
baca	read	L 8
begitu	so, in that way	C 6
bagus	good, fine	C 2
bahu	shoulder	C 5
baik	all right	L 4
baik-baik	careful	C 4
jaga baik-baik	take care	C 4
baju	blouse, jacket	C 4
baju kemeja	shirt	C 4
baju mandi	swimsuit	C 7
baju tidur	nightdress, pyjamas	C 7
bakul	basket	L 6
balik	return	L 9
bangsal	coolie lines, shed	C 2
bangun	stand up	L 8
bantal	pillow	C 5
bantal peluk	bolster	C 5
banyak	much, many	L 2
bapa	father	C 9
barang	things	C 4
barat	west	C 9
basah	wet	C 8

basuh	wash	C 8
batang	rod	L 5
batas	bank, ridge around paddy field	C 2
bau	smell	C 6
bawa	bring	L 8
bawah	under, underneath	L 9
bayam	spinach	C 2
bayar	pay	C 6
bedak	powder, cosmetic	L 9
belajar	learn	C 9
belakang	back	C 6
belas	-teen	L 3
beli	buy	L 5
belok	turn	L 8
belum	not yet	C 5
belut	eel	C 3
berapa	how much, how many	L 2
berapa banyak	how much, how many	L 2
berapa harga	what price	L 2
beras	rice, uncooked	C 2
berhenti	stop	L 8
berlanggar	accident	C 6
bersih	clean	L 1
berus	brush	C 7
besar	big	L 1
betul	correct	C 6
betulkan	to repair	C 6
bibir	lips	C 5
bidai	chicks, jalousies	C 8
biji	seed, grain	L 2
bila	when, whenever	C 6
bilah	bar (of a cage)	L 5
bilik	room	L 1
bilik tidur	bedroom	L 6
binatang	animal	C 9
bintang	star, heavenly body	C 9
biru	blue	L 1
biru tua	blue-black	C 1
bising	noise, loud	C 8
bodoh	stupid, silly	C 9
bohong	lie, tell a lie	C 8
bola	ball	L 3
boleh	able	L 6
boleh jadi	maybe	C 6
botol	bottle	C 1
buah	fruit	L 2
buah betik	papaya	L 4
buah-buahan	fruits (of all sorts in general)	C 5
buah nenas	pineapple	L 2
buang	throw away	C 8
buat	do	L 6

buatan	workmanship	C 6
budak	young boy or girl	L 6
buka	to open	C 5
bukan	no	C 1
buku	book	L 8
buku peringatan	diary	C 1
bulan	moon, month	C 4 L 6
bunga	flower	L 5
bungkus	wrap up	C 7
bunyi	sound	C 8
burung	bird	C 9
busuk	decayed	C 2
cabai	chili, long pepper	C 9
cadar	bedsheet	C 4
cakap	speak	L 8
calar	a scratch	C 6
campur	mix, mingle	C 9
cantik	pretty	L 2
cap	brand	C 1
cari	look for	L 9
cat	paint	C 6
cawan	cup	L 1
cawat	suspenders	C 7
cemburu	jealous	C10
cincang	a cut, cutting, slashing	C 3
cermat	economise	C 5
cermin	mirror	L 9
cerminmata	glasses	L 9
cerminmata hitam	sunglasses	L 9
coklat	chocolate	C 1
coli	brassiere	C 7
contoh	model	
corak	pattern	C 7
cuba	try	C 2
cuci	wash	L 4
cuci kain	wash clothes	L 4
cuci pinggan	wash dishes	L 4
cucu	grandchild	C 3
cuti	leave of absence, holiday	C 9
dada	chest (part of body)	C 5
daging	meat	L 2
dagu	chin	C 5
dah	done	C10
dahulu	before	L 4
dakwat	ink	C 1
dan	and	L 2
dapat	get, obtain	C 4
dapur	kitchen	C 7
darah	blood	C 4
dari	from	L10
daripada	from	C 5
datang	come	L 7
datuk	grandfather	C 3
daun	leaf	C 8

daun tingkap	shutter	C 8
demam	fever	C 4
dengan	with	C 9
depan	front	C 6
di	at, in	L 6
di atas	on	L 6
di balik	behind	L10
di dalam	in	L 6
di mana	where, where is	L 6
di sebelah	next door	C 3
dia	he, she	L 3
dia orang	they	L 3
dinding	partition	C 5
doktor gigi	dentist	C 4
dua	two	L 2
dua belas	twelve	L 3
dua puluh	twenty	L 3
duduk	dwell, live, sit	L 6
duit	money	L 5
ekor	tail	L 5
elok	fine	L 2
emak	mother	C 9
empat	four	L 2
enam	six	L 3
engkau	you	L 4
esok	tomorrow	L 6
fasal	concerning	C 8
fikir	think	C 6
gambar	picture	L 9
ganjil	uneven, odd	C10
gantung	hanging, suspended	L 7
garam	salt	L 5
garpu	fork	L 5
gaya	manner, tone	L 8
genap	complete, even	C10
getah	rubber	C 1
getah padam	india rubber	C 1
gigi	tooth	C 4
gincu	lipstick	L 9
goreng	fry	L 6
gula	sugar	L 5
gula-gula	a sweet	C 1
guna	use	C 7
gunakan	make use of	C 7
gunting	scissors	C 8
guru	teacher	L 8
habis	finished, done	C 4
halwa	preserves (in sugar)	C 5
hantar	convey, send	C 6
harga	price	L 2
hari	day	L 3
hari-hari	every day	L 3
hari ini	today	L 6
himpit	wedge	C 6
hendak	want, intend	C 9
hidung	nose	C 5

hijau	green	C 9
hisap rokok	to smoke (a cigarette)	L 5
hitam	black	L 2
hitung	calculate	C 9
hujan	rain	C 4
hujung	end, point	C10
hutan	jungle	C 9
ia	yes	L 2
ikan	fish	C 3
ikan pari	sting ray	C 3
ikan sembi-lang	cat fish	C 3
ikan tenggiri	mackerel	C 3
ikan yu	dog fish, shark	C 3
ikut	follow	C 7
ini	this	L 1
yang ini	this one	L 5
isi	content, filling	C 3
isteri	wife	C 2
itik	duck	C 3
itu	that, those	L 1
yang itu	that one	L 5
itu sahaja	that is all	C 1
jadi	become	C 6
jaga baik-baik	take care	C 4
jahit	sew	C 8
jalan	to go, walk, street	C 9
jam	clock, hour	L 7
jamban	W.C.	C 8
jangan	don't	L 9
jari	finger	C 5
jarum	needle	C 8
jatuh	fall, slip down	C 8
jerumat	darning	C 4
jual	sell	L 5
juga	all the same still, also	C 1
jumpa	encounter	C 4
jururawat	nurse	C 4
kacang	beans,	C 2
kacang bendi	ladies fingers	C 2
kacang boncis	French beans	C 2
kacang panjang	long beans	C 2
kacang parang	sword beans	C 2
kadang-kadang	perhaps	L 6
kah	interrogative suffix	L 7
kain	cloth	C 8
kain balut	bandage	C 4
kain dalam	under-skirt	C 7
kain lap	duster	C 7
kain sarung	sarong	C 9
kakak	elder sister	C 3

kaki	foot, leg	C 5
kalau	if	C 1
kali	time, occasion	C 1
kambing	goat, sheep	L 7
kan	See note 3	L 4
kanak-kanak	child	L 3
kanan	right	L 8
kanji	starch	C 4
kapal	ship	C 9
kapal-terbang	aeroplane	C 9
karen	eleotric current	C 8
karat	rusty	C 8
kasihan	pity	C 9
kasi	give	L 2
kata	saying, utterance	C10
katil	bed	C 5
kawan	companion, friend, party, large group of people	C 2
kayu	wood	C 1
kayu satar	ruler	C 1
ke	to	L 8
kebun	garden	L 4
kebun getah	rubber estate	C 2
kecil	small	L 1
kedai	shop	C 1
keladi	coco-yam	C 2
kelambu	mosquito net	C 5
kelapa	coconut	L 5
keledek	sweet potato	C 2
keluar	to go out	L 7
ke mana	where to	L 9
kemudian	after-wards	C 5
kena	expe-rience	C 4
kena sakit	to fall ill	C 4
kenapa	why	C 6
kepada	to	C 6
kepala	head, headman, foreman	C 4
keping	classifier for flat objects	C 3
keras	hard	C 7
kereta	car	C 6
kerja	work	L 7
kertas	paper	C 1
kertas tekap	blotting paper	C 1
kerusi	chair	L 1
ketam	crab	C 3
kiri	left	L 8
kita	we	L 5
kobis	cabbage	C 2
kosong	empty	C 9
kotak	chest, locker, container, packet	L 9

kotak bedak	powder compact	L 9
kotor	dirty	L 1
kuali	cooking pan	C 5
kuat	good, strong	C 6
kunci	lock	C 8
kuning	yellow	L 5
kupas	peel	C 4
kura-kura	tortoise	C 3
kurang	less	C 6
kurangkan	to reduce	C 6
lada	pepper	C 5
lada putih	white pepper	C 5
lagi	more	C 1
lah	emphasising suffix	L 4
lain	other, another	L 8
lain-lain	anything	C 1
laki-laki	male	L 3
lama	old, ancient, long (of time)	L 8
lambat	slow	C 9
lampu	lamp	C 6
langgar	knock against	C 6
langit	sky	C 4
lantai	floor	L 1
lapan	eight	L 3
laut	sea	C 9
layar	sail	C 9
lebam	bruise	C 4
lebih	more	L10
lebih kurang	more or less	L10
leher	neck	C 5
lekas	quick	C 9
lekuk	hollow, dent	C 6
lemak	fat, grease	C 3
lembu	bull, ox	L 7
lembut	soft,	C 7
	tender	C 7
lengan	arm	C 5
lepas	past, ago, since	C 6
lima	five	L 2
lima belas	fifteen	L 3
limau	lemon, lime, orange	C 2
lubang	hole	C 4
lobak merah	carrot	C 2
lobak putih	radish	C 2
loceng	bell	C 8
lupa	forget	L 9
macam	sort, type	C 7
madu	honey	C 3
mahal	costly, dear	C 1
mahu	to want, wish	L 4
main	play	L 3
makan	eat	L 3
makanmalam	dinner	L 7

malam	night	L 7
mana-mana	anywhere	L10
mandi	bath, bathe	C 7
mangga	mango	C 2
manggis	mangosteen	C 2
mangkuk	bowl	C 9
manis	sweet (of taste)	C 1
mari	come here	L 4
masa	time	C 6
masak	cook	C 4
masak	ripe	C 5
masam	sour	C 9
masuk	come in	L 8
mata	eye	L 9
matahari	sun	C 4
mata-mata	policeman	L 9
mata pen	nib	C 1
mati	dead	C 8
meja	table	L 1
meleleh	drip, trickle	C 8
mendaftar	register	C10
mentega	butter	C 3
merah	red	L 1
mesti	must	L 7
minggu	week	L 6
minum	drink	L 4
minuman ringan	soft drink	C 5
minyak	oil, fat	C 3
minyak babi	lard	C 3
minyak makan	cooking oil	C 3
minyak ubat	ointment	C 4
muda	young	L 8
muka	face, page	L 9
mula	start	C 9
mula-mula	firstly	L 4
mulut	mouth	C 5
muntah	vomit	C 4
murah	cheap	C 2
mutiara	pearl	C 3
naik	to mount, to go up, get up into	L 9
nama	name	L 9
nampak	see, be visible	L 9
nangka	jack fruit	C 2
nanti	wait	L 4
nasi	rice, cooked	C 2
negeri	state, country	C 9
nenek	grandmother	C 3
nya	suffix indicating possesion	L 8
nyamuk	mosquito	C 9
orang	people	L 3
orang laki-laki	man	L 3
orang perempuan	woman	L 3

orang putih	European	C 2
pada	at, by, near	L 9
padam	extinguish	C 1
padi	rice, unhusked	C 2
pagi	morning	L 6
pahit	bitter	C 1
paip air	water tap	C 8
pakai	use	L 9
pakaian	frock, dress	C 7
panas	hot	L 4
panggil	call, summon, send for	C 8
panjang	long	C 4
pasar	market	C 8
patut	right, proper	C 2
payung	umbrella	C 9
pecah	broken	L 5
pihak	party	C10
pelajaran	lesson	C 9
pendek	short	C 4
penjual	salesman	C 8
penuh	full	C 9
penyapu	broom	C 7
penyu	turtle	C 3
periksa	investigate, enquire, examine	C 4
perempuan	female	L 3
pergi	go	L 4
pergi kedai	to go shopping	C 1

perkataan	word	C 9
pernah	ever	C 2
perut	stomach	C 5
petang	evening, late afternoon	L 6
pilihanraya	election	C10
pinggan	plate	L 1
pintu	door	C 5
pipi	cheek	C 7
piring	saucer, small plate	L 1
pisang	banana	L 5
pisău	knife	L 5
pokok	tree	C 9
pokok getah	rubber tree	C 2
potong	to cut off, operate (surgical)	C 3
pukul	o'clock, strike	L 7
pulau	island	C 9
puluh	a multiple of ten	L 3
pun	used for stress and balance in the sentence	C 7
punya	own	L 9
putih	white	L 1
putus	broken, severed	C 8

rambut	hair	C 5
rasa	flavour, taste, to taste	C 2
ratus	hundred	L 3
rebus	boil	C 4
retak	cracked	L 5
ribu	thousand	L 9
ringgit	dollar	L 2
rokok	cigarette	L 5
rosak	broken, spoilt, injured	C 6
roti	bread	L 5
rugi	lose	C 1
rumah	house	L 1
rumput	grass	C 9
sabit	sickle	C 2
sabun	soap	L 4
sahaja	only	C 1
sakit	ill	C 4
kena sakit	to fall ill	
salah	fault, error	
sama	same	C 8
sampah	rubbish	C 8
sampulsurat	envelope	C 9
sana	there	L 8
saputangan	handker-chief	L 9
satar	line, stroke	C 1
satu	one	L 2
sawah	padi field	C 2
sawi-sawi	mustard	C 5

saya	I, me, my	L 1
sebelah	side	C 3
sebelas	eleven	L 3
sedap	tasty	L 4
sedikit	small, little	
sejuk	cold	L 4
sekali	once	C 1
sekeliling	position around	C 8
sekolah	school	L 1
sekolah gambar	museum	L10
selalu	always	C 6
selamat pagi	good morning	C 1
selatan	south	C 9
selsema	cold (in the head)	C 4
seluar	pants	C 7
seluar dalam	panties	C 7
seluar mandi	bathing trunks	C 7
seluar pendek	short trousers, shorts	C 4
seluar panjang	long trousers	C 4
semalam	yesterday	L 6
semangka	water melon	C 2
sembilan	nine	L 3
semua	all, the whole of, every-thing	C 1

sen	cent	L 3
senang	comfortable	C 9
sendiri	self	C 6
sengkuang	turnip	C 2
sepatu	shoes	C 7
sepuluh	ten	L 3
seterika	iron, press	C 4
setengah	half	L 7
siar	bustling about	C10
siap	ready	C 5
siapkan	to get ready	C 5
siapa	who	C 1
siapa-siapa	anybody	C 1
siku	elbow	C 5
sila	please	L 8
simpan	keep, put away	C 5
Singapura	Singapore	L 6
sini	here	L 4
sorong	push	C 8
stoking	sock, stocking	C 4
suami	husband	L 3
sudah	finished	L 7
sudah habis	done	L 7
sudah tentu	of course	C 6
sudu	spoon	L 5
suhu	temperature	C 4
suka	like	L 3
suku	quarter	
suratkhabar	newspaper	C 1
suruh	tell, give an order	L 8

susah	difficult, uneasy	C 9
susu getah	latex	C 2
tak (short for tidak)	not	L 1
tak makan	does not work	C 6
tak pernah	never	C 2
tak usah	needless	C 4
tadi	recently	L 9
tahu	know	L 7
tahun	year	L 6
takut	fear, fearful	
tali	string	C 7
talileher	tie	C 7
tali sepatu	shoelaces	C 7
tangan	hand	L 4
tangga	ladder, staircase	C 5
tanya	ask, enquire	C 5
tapi	but	L 4
tapisan	colander	C 7
tarik	pull, drag	C 8
taruh	put	L10
taugih	bean sprouts	C 2
tebal	thick	C 3
tekap	to rest the flat of the hand over anything	C 1
telur	egg	L 3
tempat	place	C 9

tengah	middle	L 7
tengahari	midday, early afternoon	L 6
tengok	look at, see	L 9
tentu	certain	C 6
tepi	edge, border	C 6
terbang	fly, flying	C 9
terima	receive, obtain	C 1
terimakasih	thank you	C 1
terlalu	surpassing, very	C 8
teruk	severe (of illness)	C 4
terung	brinjals	C 2
tiang	pillar, post	C 6
tiap-tiap	every	L 7
tidak	no	L 1
tidur	sleep	L 5
tiga	three	L 2
tikus	mouse, rat	C 8
tilam	mattress	C 5
timun	cucumber	C 2
timur	east	C 9
tingkap	window	C 5
tipis	thin	C 3
tolong	help	L 7
tolong	please	L 7
topi	hat	C 7
toreh getah	rubber tapping	C 2
tua	old	L 8
tua	deep (of colour)	C 1
tuan	master	L 5
tudung	scarf	C 7
tujuh	seven	L 3
tukang	skilled workman	C 5
tukang kebun	gardener	C 5
tukar	change, substitute,	C 8
tulang	bone	C 5
tulis	write	L 8
tunai	cash	C 7
tunjuk	show, point out	C 7
turun	descend	C 8
tutup	close	C 9
ubat	medicine	C 4
ubi kayu	tapioca	C 2
ubi kentang	potato	L 5
udang	prawn	C 3
udang galah	lobster	C 3
ular	snake	C 3
umur	age	L 8
untuk	for	C 1
utara	north	C 9
wang	money	C 6
wayang	theatrical performance	L 9
wayang gambar	pictures	L 9

yang	indicates connection between preceding and succeeding words	C 3	*yang ini*	this one, these	L 5
			yang itu	that one, those	L 5
			yang lebih	the more, the most	C 5

Suggested Translations of Exercises in the Lessons

Lesson Five (page 22)
Awak ada duit? Awak ada berapa banyak duit? Ahmad hisap rokok? Ada banyak buah nenas, tak? Ada banyak buah pisang, tak? Berapa harga sekilogram ubi kentang? Saya ada dua puluh sembilan biji ubi kentang. Ada pisau, garpu dan sudu. Saya mahu beli tiga bilah pisau. Saya tak suka cuci kain (or cuci baju or cuci kain baju).

Lesson Seven (page 28):
Pukul berapa? Saya minum teh tiap-tiap hari. Dia datang pukul enam setengah. Ini malam kita makan daging babi. Tolong datang pukul enam sepuluh minit. Tolong datang kurang lima minit pukul lapan. Saya tak suka kerja. Saya suka main-main. Ada dua biji telur. Berapa biji telur awak ada?

Lesson Nine (page 33):
Di mana saputangan awak? Ke mana awak mahu pergi? Hari ini awak pergi ke Kebun Bunga, tak? Tidak. Saya mahu pergi tengok wayang. Tolong bawa secawan air susu. Tolong ambil cawan air ini. Pagi ini ada dua orang di dalam bilik ini. Tolong carikan beg tangan saya. Silakan masuk. Suruh dia, belok ke kiri.

Lesson Ten (page 36):
Awak mahu pergi ke mana, John? Saya sudah lupa bawa cerminmata hitam saya. Tolong carikan kotak rokok saya. Adakah awak suka main-main? Kadang-kadang. Ada berapa biji cawan dan piring? Berapakah harga sebiji pinggan? Saya ada sembilan orang anak, sebuah kerusi, dua buah meja, dua

puluh biji buah nenas dan dua buah basikal. Adakah awak suka buah-buah pisang ini? Adakah buah-buah pisang itu baik? Tolong bawakan saya sedikit air panas.

NOTES

TIMES LEARN MALAY

Malay in 3 Weeks *by John Parry and Sahari Sulaiman*
A teach-yourself Malay book that enables you to communicate in practical everyday situations.

Malay Made Easy *by A.W. Hamilton*
How to speak Malay intelligibly and accurately.

Easy Malay Vocabulary: 1001 Essential Words *by A.W. Hamilton*
A handbook to enlarge your vocabulary and to ensure effective communication in Malay on a wide range of topics.

Speak Malay! *by Edward S. King*
A graded course in simple spoken Malay for English-speaking people.

Write Malay *by Edward S. King*
A more advanced course on how to read and write good modern Malay.

Learn Malay: A Phrase a Day *by Dr. G. Soosai*
A simple but comprehensive way to learn Malay in 365 days.

Converse in Malay *by Dr. G. Soosai*
A compilation of the highly successful RTM Radio Lessons series, a programme which proved both popular and beneficial to thousands of listeners in mastering Malay.

Malay Phrase Book For Tourists *by Hj Ismail Ahmad & Andrew Leonki*
The indispensable companion, it helps tourists in everyday situations in a Malay-speaking world.

Standard Malay Made Simple *by Dr. Liaw Yock Fang*
An intensive standard Malay language (bahasa Melayu baku) course designed for adult learners with no previous knowledge of the Malay language.

Speak Standard Malay: A Beginner's Guide *by Dr. Liaw Yock Fang*
An easy and comprehensive guide which enables you to acquire fluency and confidence in speaking standard Malay in only 3 months.

Malay Grammar Made Easy *by Dr. Liaw Yock Fang*
The most comprehensive guide to Malay grammar, it offers you a solid and efficient foundation to the language.

TIMES LEARN INDONESIAN

Standard Indonesian Made Simple *by Dr. Liaw Yock Fang with Dra Nini Tiley-Notodisuryo*
An intensive standard Indonesian language course designed for beginners to gain mastery of the language.

Speak Standard Indonesian: A Beginner's Guide *by Dr. Liaw Yock Fang with Drs. Munadi Patmadiwiria & Abdullah Hassan*
An easy and comprehensive guide which enables you to acquire fluency and confidence in speaking standard Indonesian in only a few months.

Indonesian In 3 Weeks *by Dr. Liaw Yock Fang with Drs. Munadi Patmadiwiria*
A teach-yourself Indonesian book that enables you to understand what people say to you, and to make yourself understood in everyday situations.

Easy Indonesian Vocabulary: 1001 Essential Words *by Dr. Liaw Yock Fang*
A handbook to enlarge your vocabulary and to ensure effective communication in Indonesian on a wide range of topics.

Indonesian Grammar Made Easy *by Dr. Liaw Yock Fang*
A companion volume to Easy Indonesian Vocabulary: 1001 Essential Words, this comprehensive book enables you to learn Indonesian with ease.

Indonesian Phrase Book For Tourists *by Nini Tiley-Notodisuryo*
A handy reference for every traveller, it helps you in everyday situations during your stay in Indonesia.

Essential Indonesian Reading: A Learner's Guide 1 *by Dr. Liaw Yock Fang & Dr. Leo Suryadinata*
Enriches learner's knowledge of contemporary Indonesian vocabulary against a backdrop of developments in its history, politics, economy, religion, culture and society.

Essential Indonesian Reading: A Learner's Guide 2 *by Dr. Liaw Yock Fang & Dr. Leo Suryadinata*
With up-to-date reading materials in Bahasa Indonesia, this book introduces students to new words especially those words used in Indonesian newspapers and periodicals. It also enriches students knowledge of contemporary Indonesia including the latest development in its history, politics, economy, religion, culture and society.

REFERENCE

Times Comparative Dictionary of Malay-Indonesian Synonyms *compiled by Dr. Leo Suryadinata, edited by Professor Abdullah Hassan*
For learners of Malay and Indonesian who want to know the differences that exist between the two languages.

Tesaurus Bahasa Melayu *by Prof. Madya Noor Ein Mohd Noor, Noor Zaini Mohd Ali, Mohd Tahir Abd Rahman, Singgih W. Sumartoyo, Siti Fatimah Ariffin*
A comprehensive A–Z thesaurus that enables you to master Malay vocabulary effectively.